THE ART
OF MATURE LOVE

CONNECTING TO OTHERS BY BEING CONNECTED TO YOURSELF

EURASIAN
CREATIVE
GUILD
LONDON

MADINA DEMIRBASH

HERTFORDSHIRE PRESS

Published in United Kingdom
FOR EURASIAN CREATIVE GUILD
Hertfordshire Press Ltd © 2017
9 Cherry Bank, Chapel Street
Hemel Hempstead, Herts.
HP2 5DE, United Kingdom

EURASIAN
CREATIVE
GUILD
LONDON

THE ART OF MATURE LOVE
CONNECTING TO OTHERS BY BEING CONNECTED TO YOURSELF

by **MADINA DEMIRBASH** ©

English

Cover design: Alexandra Rey

British Library Catalogue in Publication Data
A catalogue record for this book is available from the British Library
Library of Congress in Publication Data
A catalogue record for this book has been requested

ISBN: 978-1-910886-42-7

CONTENTS

1

ACKNOWLEDGEMENTS

First and foremost I wish to thank my beloved husband Onur Demirbash, for his continuous support at every stage of this book and my TEDx speech related to it. His kind encouragement, emotional and intellectual, nourished my creativity and inspiration. Most of the concepts which I have developed in this book emerged from conversations in our kitchen.
I also feel enormous gratitude to my curious self, forever questioning dogmas and painful beliefs, and to my lazy self, which allowed me occasional naps on the way.

I also want to thank from the bottom of my heart:

My sunny son Alparslan, for granting me a peaceful and easy pregnancy and a more joyful parenthood than I could ever have imagined;

 My dear brother Daniyar; who kept on believing in my brighter side and who despite his own challenges, helped me keep my fire burning when I needed it most – especially in the beginning. They say a rocket expends most of its energy at take-off. I received plenty of this energy from him.

Byron Katie - for revolutionizing the way I interact with people through her book: 'I Need Your Love. Is that True?' , for laying the foundation of my passion in human relationships, for granting me a scholarship to participate in the School for Work in 2015, and for one-of-a-kind unconditional love that I felt in her presence.

Nur Uner; for her encouragement to find enjoyment in the whole process, for reviewing this book.

Lyubov, our son's beloved babysitter, for her flexibility and genuine love to our precious child.

Mykola and Tatyana Latansky; for their trainings and our small chats, which inspired me and helped me acquire the tools to achieve my long-term goal, for their insightful coaching sessions.

Laura Hamilton, for her encouragement and amazing editing.

Shahsanem Murray; herself a prominent author, for consistently encouraging me to pursue my own writing.

Marat Ahmedjanov; Publisher at Hertfordshire Press, for introducing me to the world of writers in 2012 and for his support in my participation in literary competitions.

The kind staff at the library named after Ostap Vishna in Kiev; where I wrote most of the book whilst pregnant.

Valeriya Taranenko, my yoga instructor, for teaching me the art of being more attuned to my mind and body.

Hal Runkel, John Turner, and Jon Kaplan; for their support and for granting the world their beautiful 'screamfree' © teachings: a revolutionary approach to resolving conflicts.

Elchin Safarli; for his influential book: "I Was Promised to Be With You", which promised me beautifully to my husband. Our small chat during the literature forum in 2012 has opened the new gates of understanding myself.

Mariaja, Maria, Nazgul and other members of the KFCESD fund; for inviting me to lecture at their seminars about families.

Akbota and Trini; for organizing family counseling courses in Almaty, Kazakhstan. Konstantin Gonchar, my obstetrician, for his cheerful support during my pregnancy.

My psychotherapists, Serhiy Mischook and Yulia Shevchenko, for helping me find inner resources to finish this book.

Everyone who participated in my training sessions over the past ten years and raised provocative questions.

And last but not least, the picturesque streets, public art and refreshing air of my current hometown, Kiev; for a constant source of inspiration.

FOREWORD

The other day I was making one of my husband's favourite starters, yaprak sarmasi : marinated vine leaves, stuffed with rice, spices and optional minced beef, rolled into finger-sized cylinders. I thoroughly recommend it!

The rolling technique is not hard but requires time and patience, so it's always more fun to make these starters in the company of friends and family whilst sharing news and stories. Once assembled, the bundles are boiled and – voila - you have hundreds of little tastes of heaven! One day, I would like to write a cookery book for meals that I have improvised from international cuisine, but my goal for the time being, is a cookery book for everyday life, offering advice on quantities and ingredients which will provide healthy and tasty sustenance for the family. And as with food, relationships are very much influenced by what we put into them.

Adding spices and lemon or pomegranate sauce will help to add flavour but no amount of wishful thinking will ever turn rice into beans. In other words, how we enjoy marriage depends on the degree to which we are willing to work on the ingredients we put into it. No magic. No mystery. If you use rotten ingredients, how can you ever expect to produce haute cuisine? If you are unhappy in your relationship it is not because you or your partner is in the wrong but rather, the continuous use of the wrong ingredients. And if these include resentment, anger and irritation, then how can you expect a happy marriage?

This book was born from lectures that I presented to female students at vocational schools in Almaty. Together with the Kazakhstan Foundation for Social, Cultural, and Educational

Development[1] we aimed to show them what lay beyond the curtain of the wedding

Ceremony and suggest ways in which they could find long-term happiness in marriage. In short: to break through the romantic myths which surround intimate relationships and to motivate these women to work on establishing a fulfilling family life from the outset. Other sources for the book include individual and group consultations conducted with clients and friends, characters and plots from selected books and films, and my own personal experience. This book was born from the urge to structuralize the everyday work required for a happy marriage . Yes, you read it correctly! Every- Day- Work. This book should be read as a job description of sorts and the contract you are about to sign is with your higher Self. The harder you work, the better the 'pay', and there will be bonuses too, in the form of something far beyond love: inner strength and peace. This guide is intended for everyone, regardless of personal circumstances and whether or not they are in a relationship.

 Please do not be misguided by the word "marriage" in this book since it was not my intention to use it in the literal or conventional sense. I follow instead, the teachings of Byron Katie, Eckhart Tolle, and the Mooji school of thought that equates marriage with security for the Ego. No piece of paper or 'label' can guarantee true intimacy between two people, and conversely, cannot prevent people from separating from each other physically or emotionally. You might question my stance since here I am, bound in marriage to my sweetheart, but I should add that I entered that state long before I understood the illusion of the marriage certificate.

I should also admit that I struggled with the social pressure to legalize our relationship through marriage instead of us being free to simply set up home together.

---

[1] www.kazfond.kz

What is done is done. Most importantly, neither of us views our marriage certificate as any type of guarantee. Thus, when I refer to 'marriage', I mean any form of relationship to which a couple, regardless of gender, is committed.

Each chapter of this book includes a theoretical section, illustrated by examples from real life consultations, and a section for self-reflection in which the reader is asked to respond to questions. I have also included questions for couples to answer at the end of each chapter. These are designed to help you to identify areas which require discussion and ultimately lead to a better understanding of each other's' needs and a stronger relationship. And unexpectedly for myself, I decided to include the "When I explain it to my son, when he turns five years" section at the end of every chapter.

At the very end of the book, there is a section for taking notes, or logging any insights gleaned while applying aspects of this guide to your life. In a way it is a work book, which will help you to stay on track and identify areas that require your attention or work in order to manifest the desired results.

This book is for you and you alone; not your friend nor your parent, and not for god's sake, your partner. One of its most important principles, reiterated time and again, is that the process outlined always starts and ends with you. Ultimately, you cannot control other people, no matter how much you want to, and as soon as you accept that no-one needs to change for your sake, your frustration in trying to govern their lives, will abate.

Nowadays, books and articles on how to manipulate your partner into particular actions remain ever popular and yes, their techniques can be effective. However, in most cases, it is only your ego that benefits. Whenever you shift your focus on anyone or anything beyond yourself and begin to identify faults and necessary ' improvements', you immediately find yourself trapped in a swamp instead of in a river which can be crossed.

That swamp, which bogs you down, is your ego. Whenever you manipulate your partner into doing something, there will always be some other dissatisfying trait that needs to be changed, and then another and another, always leaving you disappointed. Moreover, I know from my own experience, that manipulation, however subconscious, always carries a fear of being discovered. Remember, what I wrote about cooking with rotten ingredients? Lies and deception added to the ingredients of your relationship will always leave a bitter aftertaste...However, the choice is yours and it may well be that you have found manipulation an effective and fulfilling component of your relationship, which works for both parties.

If so, my book is not for you!

This book or job description if you like, is for those who are ready to work on themselves; for this is the only road that will lead to lasting change. Action is what is needed to activate that famous law of attraction, backed by positive thinking and affirmation of intent. I decided to take action and write this book, for my goal is helping people rediscover and develop their ability to love and in doing so, unleash their full potential as human beings, partners and parents. I have long observed miserable couples and singles and up until a few years ago, I too found myself riding a long road of suffering and desperation. This book is intended to help you leave that road by way of a shortcut and so save your time and energy for doing something great in the world: spreading love. It does not have to be within a marriage and indeed, I am not advocating a married life over a single one. The book should prove particularly helpful to anyone thinking about committing to a relationship either now or in the future and will also benefit those who choose to remain single and dedicate their lives to a cause.

One last word before we begin our journey: be gentle on yourself. Please do not analyze either the advice offered or the suggested exercises as if studying for an exam. Try to avoid falling into common traps. I frequently have difficulty in accepting my current circumstances and begrudged, find it difficult to move on. Before making a move towards my goal, I find myself trying to justify my actions and thinking about what has stopped me from taking any action until now.

It's as if there's a voice of a demanding parent living inside my head. There are times when she takes over the steering wheel and when she sees fit to scold rather than offer gentle encouragement. She is not particularly smart, but nor is she stupid. One day, she simply adopted this role and since then, has become very good at it. Why is it so important to acknowledge her presence? If you happen to have such small sub-personality inside your head, then please let her speak and let off steam but do not let her voice paralyze your progress through the exercises. She may try to convince you that because your goal is so far out of reach, you will never attain it or she may focus your attention on the weaker sides of your character that you should have dealt with long ago. My advice to you is to participate in these exercises out of curiosity, rather than shame or guilt. And play with that little woman in your head!

My goal is to help people rediscover and develop their ability to love and in that unleash their full potential as human beings, partners, and parents.

FINDING YOUR CHAIR

I remember once at university, back when I was a sophomore, coming across a member of staff who had married a few months previously. Out of politeness, I asked her how she was enjoying married life, fully expecting the usual retort: "It is hard, but worth it," or "They say it's always difficult at the beginning". Instead, I was astonished to hear her say: "Marriage is so cool!" Her eyes shone like never before and it was clear that she meant what she said! Part of me still questions whether she was faking it and I knew nothing about her family but it struck me that she was the first person I'd ever heard enthuse about how she was enjoying that new stage of her relationship. We didn't speak for long but for years it left me wondering whether there could be a better way to live in a relationship. What does it take to make a happy marriage? Why do so many people suffer within marriage? Why do they get divorced? Is divorce a solution to a difficult marriage?

I started looking for answers, and due to my state of mind, discovered attaching to the external circumstances to be the key, especially when leading to loneliness and despair. This realization was confirmed in the spiritual teachings of Byron Katie, Deepak Chopra and Oprah Winfrey, and research undertaken by professional family psychologists Hal Runkel, Prof. Dr. D. Javier Escriva Ivars and other professionals. Essentially, everything in my life in the past, present and future begins with me, not with the external circumstances. As soon as I had embraced this concept, I began to notice all sorts of remarkable transformations in my relationships with family, friends and people around me.

My challenge almost two years ago was to share this sweet discovery with female adolescents attending vocational classes in Almaty, as part of an international project. I came up with seven answers for the question of how to have a happy marriage. My husband and I then developed our theory, after he asked me to find a simple metaphor on which to pin these seven recommendations. We were in the kitchen at the time and I remember searching the room for a familiar object which could embody these ideas. Dismissing the table, fridge and microwave as unsuitable, I felt a rush of excitement when I noticed that the chair had seven sides. It was an obvious choice and almost immediately, I realized that an analogy with 'Musical Chairs' would provide a fun way to explore this theory[2].

The next day I gave my first lecture in Almaty. When asked why people get married, most of the class provided predictably, positive responses including: "Because they love each other"; "To have children legally", or "Because it's traditional." I then asked why they thought people got divorced. After an initial silence, there came a few hesitant replies: "Money issues?" "Mismatched personalities?" "Relatives?" In order to illustrate the key answer to that question, I asked 6 participants to come onto the stage and in pairs, run around three chairs. The format was similar to 'Musical Chairs' except in this instance, I asked each 'couple' to only run around one chair. I also placed another set of three chairs within their sight and reach. When the music stopped, there were three possible outcomes for the participants:

---

[2] The basic rules of 'Musical Chairs' are as follows: The number of participants exceeds the number of chairs by one. Participants are asked to run around these chairs, while the music is playing. As soon as it stops, they are supposed to sit down on a chair. The person left without a seat leaves the game and takes one chair with them. The game continues in the same manner until there are only two people who must compete for one chair.

- Two were sitting side by side on one chair
- One was sitting and one was standing
- One was sitting on the lap of the other

As fun as it was, they soon grew sad and pensive as they tried to grasp the meaning behind the metaphor: most people enter marriage without a "chair", since nobody told them NOT to take one with them. In my experimental game, I placed a further three chairs within a few metres of the three set up in the centre of the stage. When the music stopped and they were sitting awkwardly on their chairs or standing nearby, I showed them the other three chairs that they could have requested or moved of their own accord.

I had said nothing against them taking one of these chairs yet none of them had even tried and thus had not questioned what they perceived to be the rules of the "unhappy marriage" game. Alas, there are too many people playing it like this for real, without realizing the consequences.

And so, the initial reasons for getting married – love and support for each other – are lost and marriage becomes a competition about who can grab the seat first. It's no wonder that the couple end up quarrelling or maintaining cold, hostile silences as they harbor bitterness for each other. They then end up getting divorced or out of fear of loneliness or abject criticism, tolerating an unhappy marriage. How could they not? There is a lack, a perpetual lack, of something they could have taken to the marriage in the first place; something barely mentioned in our culture. We are conditioned to believe that through marriage, your partner will provide you with something which is missing from your life. We also think that a happy marriage is exemplified by the wedding celebration rather than how we cope with the obligations and responsibilities which begin when we sign by the marriage certificate. They say that love is about giving. But how can you give something you don't have? How can you share your chair, when all you think about is how you tired you are of standing and want to sit down? We are continuously told that all we need a prince or a princess, but all we need is a chair!

So what does our chair stand for? In this instance, it is a symbol of maturity. People get divorced or stay in miserable marriages because they have not taken maturity into their union. I came up with the term **machairity** (maturity + chair) level. They hope that now and then, their partner will allow them to sit on their chair, if indeed they have one! They don't realize that if they are able to construct their own chair, independent of their partner, they are much more likely to be happy in a committed relationship. We are living in an era when we expect a 'quick fix' for everything but simply saying 'I do' at the altar will never guarantee happiness. Maturity is not so much a destination as a principle, a state of mind, and a desire to grow.

A chair is made up of many parts so if it represents maturity, we must ensure that each part is properly maintained so that it serves us well. Otherwise, any ensuing imbalance may cause it to collapse and cause us discomfort and pain.

Why a rocking chair? For me it is something that offers both fun and a sense of calm; two emotions which I hope you will experience while reading this book. It is also like a pendulum, which can gently stop and bring you into the now – a place of power, insight, understanding, and acceptance of reality. As Eckhart Tolle says, contrary to popular belief, our purpose in life is not to provide some grandiose meaning for humanity. That is secondary. Our primary purpose is being present. Later I will explain how powerful that is for relationships, especially the one you have with yourself.

I don't claim to have discovered anything new but instead, have enjoyed playing around and reinterpreting previous findings. So be prepared to digest familiar concepts cooked in an unfamiliar sauce.

We are continuously told that all we need a prince or a princess, but all we need is a chair!

Picture 1. Machairity

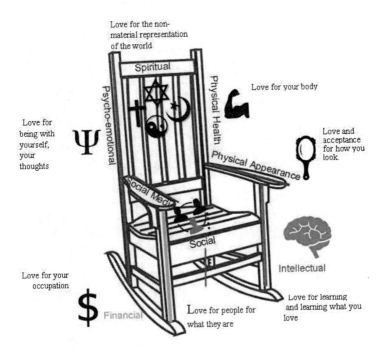

Table 1. How different parts of the chair affect different areas in our lives

Maturity	You Personally	In relationships	In raising children
Psycho-emotional[3]	Connecting to yourself , develop your integrity, learn to love yourself unconditionally	Connecting to a person based on love, not fear or need of approval	Connecting to your child and enjoying precious moments rather than struggling over authority
Physical health[4]	Making you follow your dreams more effectively with higher energy level	Sustaining sexual activity and endorphins (happiness hormones) Up	For women: increasing the chances of giving birth easier. (For both men and women): increasing energy to take a better and kinder care of small children.[5]

---

[3] Recommeded authors: B.Katie, E.Tolle, H.Runkel, Louise Hay, W. Dyer, Mooji, G.Chapman
[4] Recommeded authors: A.Robbins, J. Mercola, L.Bourbeau, L.Hay, J.Vitale, C.Tipping, D.Servan-Schreiber, J.Ortner
[5] As Dr. Komarovsky says, the best parents are the rested parents.

Intellectual maturity[6]	Staying interesting for yourself; bringing joy from learning about the topic you have genuine passion about	Promoting creativity in problem-solving; keeping brain open to new ideas	Nourishing children's intellectual interests, helping them reach their potential
Financial[7]	Paying for healthy food and for other self-development activities	Giving you freedom to enter, stay, or leave a relationship	Paying for the best education and other developmental activities of your child
Social[8]	Creating the most powerful antidote to depression;	Becoming a friend for your partner and for his/her relatives and friends, regardless of who they are	Making true friends with your child

---

[6] You are welcome to choose authors of your interest
[7] Recommeded authors: H.Ecker, N.Latansky, N.Hill, J.Vitale, M.Sinetar, J.Canfield
[8] Recommended authors: S.Harley, B.Katie, E.Tolle, H.Runkel

Spiritual[9]	Feeling connected to the world and to every moment of it	Seeing your partner as God's child, innocent and worthy of love every moment	Taking care of your child just as the Universe is taking care of you - gently and lovingly
Appearance [10]	Discovering real beauty in yourself, which in turn helps seeing it everywhere and in everyone.		

One of the other benefits of constructing and developing your own chair is that you start noticing and attracting other people who have chairs. You will think twice before committing to a relationship with a "chair-less" person and should always resist the temptation to construct a chair for them. Only he or she can know what is best for them and your hard work will be in vain. It is like push-ups - nobody can do them for you. I remember being asked at a lecture: "What if I met my husband when he was completely chair- less, and I constructed one for him within our marriage?" The answer came to me much later, I wanted to ask her, "Is he happy with the chair you constructed for him? Are you fulfilled with yours? Did you spend most of your energy constructing his chair or truly loving each other?" Many of us like to feel like heroes, yet we forget to fight in the right field - in our own mind, not someone else's.

---

[9] Recommended authors: B.Katie, E.Tolle, the main books of religions, J. Moses

[10] Recommended authors: J. Ortner, L.Chaouli,V. Konovalova

Another frequent question I'm asked is: "If someone is fully mature and self-sufficient, why would they bother with a relationship?" Well, wouldn't it be nice to enter into a relationship out of curiosity, rather than the need to fill an imaginary gap? When two people who have already reached maturity get together, that intimate contact with one another makes them more open to a deeper understanding of themselves and how they relate to the world. Just like this book, its value becomes known through reading rather than sitting on a shelf. Interaction with others offers us a reflection of who we are, through the eyes of our 'readers'.

But why are we hesitant about giving it a try? Could it be something in our early programming?

Many of us like to feel like heroes, yet we forget to fight in the right field - in our own mind, not someone else's.

THE IMPORTANCE OF THE CHAIR IN A CHAIR-FREE SOCIETY

To understand further what I mean by maturity, I want to show you what it is not, and how our culture is promoting a 'chair-less' society. Maturity is love in its broadest sense; for the world in which we live, our fellow human beings, nature, our occupations, and most importantly, for those things that challenge our ability to love. Love means being able to surrender to the moment and being at peace with the world. Mature love is not dispelled by adverse circumstances.

I have made a long and difficult journey from being a dependent, hungry and scared "child" to a happily married woman. I learned how to take myself from the state of a unhappy demand to a 'happy' destination by learning how to identify the internal reason for my unhappiness and then feeling positive about working on it. And if I managed to complete this journey, then other people can too. A lack of mature love may lead to marital discontent but I believe that its roots lie in unhealthy early childhood programming.

Throughout our childhood, we are bombarded with the notion that marriage is about getting something that you cannot possibly give yourself, and this is reiterated by the lives of fictional female characters. Let's look at the messages portrayed. In 'Cinderella' we are taught that there is no profit in working on relationships with our siblings and instead, we should tolerate our poor circumstances until some kind fairy magically appears to sort out our problems. Cinderella herself is unfulfilled both intellectually and spiritually and has no outlet for her creativity. She also lacks inner peace so how can the fairy ever expect her to have a truly happy marriage with the prince? What ingredients is she bringing to the meal? In her new role as a princess, she'll even be deprived of the job she did well and in the best case scenario, may find herself feeling disenfranchised. Naturally none of this is explored in a story which focuses on marriage as the ultimate means by which this young woman can escape misery. And after the wedding, when reality hits, where will the fairy be then?

Regrettably, many people leap into marriage without any thought about how they will cope with the inevitable, often adverse, changes to their lives and in the absence of a kind fairy, expect their parents to 'sort things out'.

Let's look at another popular fairy tale, which thankfully, has been more critically scrutinized by experts. "Sleeping Beauty" programmes us to believe that finding a 'perfect match' or 'the one' (something non-existent in our universe) is a matter of pure luck. You happen to fall asleep, or in reality remain invisible, until as a consequence of your beauty, your perfect man finds you. You don't need to develop yourself or learn how to address your problems. In fact you don't need to do anything at all except lie down and wait. The story's message to men is equally detrimental since it involves no active role on their behalf other than find a passive, unhappy sleeping beauty and marries her right away.

And then there's Thumbelina, who finds herself unhappily entangled in the world of animals and insects because she didn't take time to discover herself. I am not saying we shouldn't use adventure as a means of self-discovery but in contrast to Thumbelina's situation, it should always be a conscious choice. We learn nothing about her interests or passions, only her misery. Towards the end she finally manages to shake off her sadness by learning to serve others – starting by taking care of a bird- and thus intuitively, begins to develop her spiritual maturity. However, Thumbelina does not find real happiness until she meets her prince and once again the message, so deeply rooted in our culture, is clear: If you are miserable, find a partner, and you will live happily ever after. But what exactly can they offer one another and what have they done to prepare for this union so that it will survive and flourish beyond 'love at first sight'?

I am not claiming that young children should become familiar with sources and details of marital discord but that they should be given an idea of what makes a happy relationship. Luckily, there is one fairy tale that serves as a fine example: 'Beauty and the Beast'. Belle, the main female character, is well-read (intellectual maturity) makes friends easily and is compassionate towards her father (social maturity), and most importantly, has an ability to express love (psycho-emotional maturity). She assists her father in his business, thus learning how to make money (financial maturity), and leads an active life (physical health). She spends time on her appearance without obsessing about it (physical appearance), and she sees beyond superficial appearance, beauty behind anger and magic in the ordinary (spiritual maturity). As a result of her maturity on all levels, she is able to love the Prince for who he is; one of the most challenging tasks in marriage. To my mind, the story would have been better if she had used her interest in literature to initiate a writing or poetry project; something which would have harnessed her gift and provided a source of income, since no kingdom's wealth is ever guaranteed!

It's a pity indeed, that most classic fairy tales end with their main characters overcoming their difficulties and getting married. As we grow older, this theme is further perpetuated by Hollywood movies and pop music, continuously promoting romance but rarely exploring what comes next.

Concurrently, in the real world, we are surrounded by less than perfect scenarios in which families exist in hostile worlds, filled by hatred and disrespect. Amidst such conflict, the divorce rate soars, ending almost 50% of marriages. Such discord is naturally open to dramatic interpretation but cheating and other related scandals presented in films and on TV are rarely resolved in a healthy way and more often than not, lead to tragedy. And so our confusion and disconnection from alternative, more constructive answers, grows daily.

We are so attracted to the idea of becoming happily married, but much less so with staying in a happy marriage. Why, we wonder, are the promises made by fairy tales not fulfilled? Well, could it be because no one told us to grow up or told us that we had to construct our own chair?

I knew none of this and suffered as a result. It took me at least 22 years to understand that I had to grow up. Growing can be painful, but remaining immature in the adult world is even more hurtful. Ever since I remember, I've heard and said the words "I love you", without ever thinking about what they mean. I love you, if you love me? Why do I love you? Is it for this or for that? Am I lovable? (I was 25 years old before I felt convinced). How can I make you love me? Is there such a thing as platonic love? How can I make myself attractive to the opposite sex? My search for answers began in elementary school, when I had my first crush on my brother's classmate. It remained with me through dates in high school and then casual, 'junk food', relationships until I was 24. I couldn't see any prospect of finding a meaningful relationship. In an attempt to find answers, I spent four years studying psychology but rather than help, it drove me to question how my parents had brought me up the way they did. I diagnosed myself with many disorders and was stuck with blaming my mother and father for not giving me enough love in my childhood. Over years of searching for, and failing in, "love" affairs, I had unwittingly struggled to embrace one fundamental issue: The chair must be unique and fit the needs of an individual and thus cannot be obtained or constructed by anyone else but you. I had been looking for love in the wrong place: outside myself. I was so hungry for that external love, that I was ready to make any kind of sacrifice; something which I later regretted. I remember feeling so lonely and unlucky in love that I would cry for hours. Trying to sit on someone else's chair was a lose-lose deal.

How can one person give another, something they don't even possess? It is no coincidence that chair-less people attract each other but even if a person with a chair is attracted to a chair-less one, their affair cannot last long. I have been unhappy when single and in a relationship.

No wonder we are so attracted to the idea of becoming happily married, but much less so in maintaining a happy marriage. We wonder why the fairy tale is not fulfilled. Could it be because no one told us to grow up?

When I was single I felt the lack of something profoundly important, which I believed could only be filled with someone else's love, or a relationship. But whenever I managed to catch someone in my net (and believe me; I worked really hard), I still felt down. That empty gap in my life wasn't being filled. It all seemed so hopeless and I began to think that due to bad luck, I was destined to suffer forever. Eckhart Tolle claims that we must first experience suffering in order to understand that we don't need to, and indeed, this is what happened to me.

Growing up, becoming mature, or building your chair so to speak, does not mean that you never ask anything of your partner. Yet there is a vast difference between wanting something that will complement or enhance your life, and wanting something to validate it. As a married woman, I want be loved, feel beautiful, feel connected, be listened to, and most of all – accepted, but I do not need these things. Can I claim to be happy now simply because I was happy before my marriage? No: I am now happier because I grew up and actually continue to grow, for marriage like nothing else, demands my growth and brings joy from the wisdom of seeing an expanded picture of love and peace. Marriage, if you work on it, brings you closer to your natural sense of being and pure unconditional love for that is. It also highlights areas on which a little more work would help us become more loving and kind.

Questions for self-reflection

Do I see entering into a relationship/marriage as a solution to my current unhappiness/lack of something?

Am I guaranteed that I will receive these things in marriage?

I hope that it is now becoming clearer why people get divorced. They hope for compensation and a cover up for their feelings of emptiness, their wounds, and their failings. It is very much a consumerist approach which whilst very efficient, lasts only for a short time: time to see the wedding through but not long enough for a happy marriage.

The happiest married people are people whose marriages were based on choice rather than need, as my teacher Hal Runkel says, and I couldn't agree more. They are as happy on their own as with their spouses. They enjoy a freedom of choice – fundamental to a successful marriage - to love, give, support, receive and learn. It's something which I shall be encouraging and nurturing in my son, before and especially when he turns five years, for the most creatively free and confident child is the one who can play with or without toys.

PSYCHO–EMOTIONAL MATURITY

People [myself included] are just as wonderful as sunsets if you let them be. When I look at a sunset, I don't find myself saying, "Soften the orange a bit on the right hand corner." I don't try to control a sunset. I watch with awe as it unfolds.
Carl Rogers

Today I understood what had been the greatest shift in my relationships with my husband. It happened, when I realized that my respect for him cannot depend on his actions. I kept on waiting for him to live up to my expectations and so earn my respect. But he never did. And nor was he obliged to do so. It was matter of freedom of choice and not a condition of love. Neither love nor respect are things that people have to earn from me. I want to offer both, regardless of how they behave, for my own sake and sanity. Because when I learnt how to give freely to others, I made the greatest gift to myself. If I happen to receive love in return, I feel thankful; if I don't I also feel thankful for that other person has shown me that they are not yet ready for our friendship. Do I get angry at a tree because it sheds its leaves in winter? Do I take that personally? No! Then why take people's reactions personally? And moreover, why get upset by actions taken by me against myself?

 Psycho-emotional maturity is one of my favourite topics, because of the way it challenges me. I understand the how, but do not always practice it. The most important thing is that I am developing, and looking back, I am amazed b y how far I've come. I have learned how to switch from an ever-unhappy consumer to an abundant giver of love and acceptance.

I have become more mature but still have much to achieve; one step at a time.

So what does this psycho-emotional part of the chair stand for? I define it as

being able to deal with your psyche through love; our most important emotion.

Psyche, according to the Merriam-Webster dictionary, is "the soul, mind or personality of a person or a group". I will talk more about the soul in my chapter on spiritual maturity. But I have problems with the concept of personality because it presupposes some kind of identity that our ego is eager to hold on to and then use to disconnect us from the rest of the world. Thus, I choose to concentrate on the mind aspect of the psyche which I regard as the biggest obstacle to our reaching maturity. So, once again, in simple terms: psycho-emotional maturity means to love your own mind.

Unless I learn this skill, I will keep on projecting my inner conflicts on other people, relentlessly blaming them for my unhappiness. So what is my mind at the end of the day? You will be surprised to hear that it pertains to everything that's going on outside me, rather than something within me! It is a space containing thoughts with which I have erroneously learned to identify myself: "I AM worried", "I don't believe you", "I AM hurt", and so on. As Byron Katie says, "If you were your mind (thoughts), then who is the one noticing your thoughts?" To further comprehend the separation of mind and observer, I found it helpful to listen to Eckhart Tolle's story. On the verge of committing suicide, he announced "I cannot live with myself anymore". And that moment of dis-identification was immediately followed by the question: "Who is the self and who is ' I 'that cannot live with it?"

Questions for self-reflection

What are your thoughts on this topic?

Can you see that they live outside you?

So who are YOU?

_____

You (or your true nature) are the person who existed before you started believing your thoughts. This natural being, comprising love and light, has nothing to do what you have or haven't done or your achievements, places you've been to, or how many likes you accrue on social networks. So as I see it; there is a natural you and someone constructed from all sorts of beliefs about you. As these beliefs entered your sphere, your mind happened to identify with them. They are not real and neither are the events that spawned them. When you learn to dis-identify from them, you get to see the real you, and loving yourself and others becomes inevitable. You cannot truly love someone without loving your natural self; nor can you really get to know someone until you know yourself. No matter how many relationships you have, none will fulfil you until you develop a loving relationship with yourself and your thoughts. I am no spiritual teacher, just a follower of those who have attained a profound peace of mind. Their ideas strongly resonate with my inner intuitive knowledge. Their philosophies have enabled them to help thousands of people around the globe by teaching them how to free themselves from suffering and thereafter, form happy relationships. By first transforming their relationships with themselves and their thoughts, it is possible for anyone to change their relationships with the rest of the world for good. Many manage to attain this separation form the mind through reading or listening to spiritual teachers but for others, it is more difficult. If you are one of the latter, then let's see if I can help you to get closer to this state. The separation is important because it makes the process easier, much in the same way that it's easier to alter a dress when you're not wearing it. The first step is to focus on what is going on in your head and a good way to begin this process, is to shut yourself off from everything around you by simply concentrating on your breathing.

Sometimes in order to find the answers, it helps to identify what they are not.

This is particularly true when seeking happiness. When I recognize the thoughts that are causing my unhappiness, I gradually come to see how I can make myself happy ; whether by taking action, by surrendering to a situation, or walking away from it. Throughout years of searching and practice, I have found that the best method for me is the 'Work' advocated by Byron Katie. It helps to me to identify stressful thoughts, then work with them and let them go, and moreover, attain a sense of freedom through them. I invite you to visit thework.com for more information but meanwhile, ask you to complete the judge-your-neighbor worksheet, which you can find on http://thework.com/sites/thework/downloads/worksheets/JudgeYourNeighbor_Worksheet.pdf

For many of my clients, the simple act of filling out the questionnaire provided them with a sense of relief. Let's play with it now. Let's learn how we can work with our thoughts and mind by listing anything we think we need from other people. But most importantly, let's see how we react, when we dispel all thought that we need these things from others. The most common needs that I frequently hear are: approval of beauty/intellect/charm, security, support, surprise, loyalty, love, admiration, understanding, listening, connection, compassion, acceptance, etc.

Questions for self- reflection

Remember one specific situation, when one of the below needs was not met by your partner/ friend/parent and you felt frustrated: approval of beauty/intellect/charm, security, support, surprise, loyalty, love, admiration, understanding, listening, connection, compassion, and acceptance.

Take 10-30 minutes to fill out the Judge-Your-Neighbour Worksheet with reference to a specific situation. Choose one of the statements, which best reflects the pain you felt. Underline it then challenge it with the four questions. For example: My husband should be more compassionate towards me. Only after I have answered the four questions, I am ready to tackle a turnaround and in this case, realized that it is I who must show myself more compassion. If I jump to the turnarounds right away, my mind will be more resistant and superficial. I then need to think about how I can do this, and found the answer in following Oprah Winfrey's and Deepak Chopra's meditation on compassion and self-compassion. I could also reference the Dalai Lama's excellent and very accessible lectures on compassion. Other people may prefer to seek compassion through prayer. For my husband, an ultimate feeling of compassion is found in being listened to. So when he needs it, he either listens to himself – through writing or recording his thoughts - or asks me to listen to him. Whatever the issue, take your time and focus deeply.

For another, more detailed example of a completed worksheet, please refer to the Appendix, where I worked through the notion: My husband should surprise me with gifts. It is always fun to notice how I react to different issues and what transpires in the turnarounds to make me feel fulfilled. It is like stepping through the Looking Glass and beyond. It's a completely different universe - unknown, peaceful, loving. In a matter of 20-30 minutes I am now able to turn hatred into genuine love and gratitude.

The Work of Byron Katie is like stepping through the Looking Glass and beyond. It's a completely different universe - unknown, peaceful, loving.

For me, I would consider you emotionally mature, if you are able to reconnect with your ability to love yourself, your neighbour, and your "here and now". Why love, rather than another emotion? Because love is something to which we will naturally, always turn. It is the foundation of peace of mind, achievement, the realization of our potential, and taking care of ourselves and our relationships. It does not mean that other emotions don't matter or are less valid. Naming them and acknowledging them is important, if only to let them guide you back to love, i.e. to your natural state. Every part of the maturity chair contains love or an essence of it. Indeed, the main component of the chair as a whole is love. Psycho-emotional maturity is also about doing what you love, which makes you feel loved and enormous fun can be had in giving love to the world. Love is also closely related to creativity which is why Freud named our creative instinct 'Eros', from the ancient Greek for love or desire. By creating something, you naturally and subconsciously, become a more loving person.

Another incidental benefit of doing what you love is that it:
- Increases your energy level (physical health),
-   Develops your intellect: studying something you love becomes much more fun (intellectual maturity);
-   Leads you towards areas where you could make the most money (financial maturity);
- Lights up your eyes in a way which cannot be achieved with make-up (appearance in real life and social media)
- Connects you with like-minded people and expands your social network (social maturity).

In a recent discussion with a friend, he asked why bother trying to discover your "project" and follow its path, when there is no guarantee that it is yours or that it will bring you satisfaction in the end? The answer immediately sprung to mind: Because embarking on your project makes you feel truly connected to God, the Universe, or something else which is far bigger and mightier than you. You become more spiritually mature. You feel like your inner dots have been connected; a transcendental feeling of inner integrity and peace. It cannot be bought or borrowed from anyone. It can only be experienced by following your path.

What you love is part of who you are and part of global project of making the world a better place. For instance, I love taking pictures and editing them. I believe it helps me see the beauty

of the world and things that I had previously overlooked[11].
Most importantly, it helps me be in the present moment.
Some people love fashion and others, animals: the object of
our love is immaterial just as there are no limits to what we
can do with love or how we can expand love in the world.

Please list 7 things that you love to do on the left and how
each can benefit others on the right.

1.

2.

3.

4.

5.

6.

7.

Which of the above could you do within the next 36 hours?

When you realize your potential or do something
that you love, you feel truly connected to God,
the Universe or something far bigger and mightier
than you. You feel like your inner dots have finally
been connected. You feel like "you are not the
drop in the ocean, but the ocean in a drop" as
Rumi says.

---

[11] www.madination.com

Now that we have talked about Love, let's turn to its opposite: Fear. This is what usually prevents us from following our passion or from entering or leaving relationships. I know it too well, for I have been riddled with it for years with my previous boyfriends, if I can call them this way. I remember being afraid of making the wrong impression, losing his respect/love/attention or losing him to another, prettier girl. Above all, I was afraid of rejection once he had discovered my imperfections and my deep-rooted feeling of inadequacy. At times I was so afraid that I could not talk properly. In such a state of mind there is little place for love, if any. And that is all right. At times, fear can be our best teacher, if we allow it to be. For a long time I was afraid to take up psychology. I lacked confidence in my own capabilities and was sure that no-one would take me seriously. I was afraid of making mistakes. Little did I know that in order to avoid making mistakes, I had to dispel all fear and instead, continuously develop my specialist knowledge.

Let's talk about the fear of losing someone's love. As Eckhart Tolle claims in "Stillness Speaks", a good place to start is to recognize that nothing in life is permanent. Everything is ultimately, as transient as the air we breathe. But let's say that's too hard for your ego to accept; an understandable situation given the fact that the ego is enhanced by illusionary possessions. The ego is also enhanced by not being in the present, but in some still unborn future. Let's bring it back to reality. If you think about it, most of our fears never materialize but what is always a certainty, is our ability to picture the most terrifying scenarios which then destroy our peace of mind. We often think that we could never handle the worst yet end up 'dancing in the rain'. Thirdly, fear paralyses action, even the most simple or necessary. I recall being so terrified of losing a seemingly perfect boyfriend, that whenever he paused in conversation or used the phrase "I need to tell you something", I could hardly breathe for fear of being told he was breaking up with me.

Instead of talking to him openly about the obvious problems in our relationship, my fears, my feelings, I unconsciously chose to remain silent. In fact, I was so afraid of potentially losing him and being left alone, that I started seeing another man.

And over the years, I've heard about too many clients cheating on their spouses for the same reason: the fear of losing even a little piece of love.

Before too long, my ex-boyfriend actually said "I am sick of you" and initiated our break-up. Fear did not help me to sustain that relationship and undoubtedly contributed to its gradual destruction.

The more training I receive, the more I learn about different methods of dealing with fear. Back in 2011, an effective method that helped me tremendously was the Emotional Freedom Technique. Covered in a wide range of literature and videos on the internet, this method involves tapping specific points of your face and body, while speaking out your negative emotions and then replacing them with related positive statements. It is actually very simple, yet profound, for it brings a release and provides clarity of mind; both of which enable you to take necessary action. I found the best instructors on an online World Tapping Summit; an annual event organized by Jessica and Nick Ortner. This method has helped thousands of people around the globe and might well become your favourite tool[12].

There is a short introduction to the method, which I like sourced from the official tapping website link http://www.thetappingsolution.com/what-is-eft-tapping/

Alternative methods include writing down your fears. In many respects, this can prove more effective, for it activates your thinking process and by creating a tangible, written list you

---

[12] www.theTappingSolutions.com

literally have to 'face' your fears. Moreover, studies undertaken by Forbes[13] at Indiana University have shown that handwriting "increases neural activity in certain sections of the brain, much like meditation." I first read about writing down your fears in Joe Vitale's "The Key", immediately followed by Bryan Tracy's "Psychology of Achievement", and I recently heard about a similar method being employed by Myola Latansky, who has learned it from

Marcia Weider. She suggests that we deal with our fears by writing ALL of them down, without any filtering, and then dividing them into two types: fears based on beliefs and fears based on actions. Fears based on beliefs vary from person to person but some of the most common include: "I am unlovable", "Life is unfair", "Men/women only want one thing", etc.

Fears based on action are equally varied but are frequently expressed in statements such as: "If I date this guy, he will break my heart"; "If I speak my mind, my boyfriend will break up with me"; "If I commit to a relationship, I will sacrifice my freedom", etc. The simple act of putting your fears in writing is a form of release since at the very least; it allows you to start seeing what you are working with. Secondly, when you divide your fears into two categories, you will see that there is a different way to approach them. One way of dealing with fears based on beliefs can be replacing them with the alternative, positive statements and then think about how realistic these are. For example, you replace "Life is unfair" with "Life is fair" or "Men only want one thing" with "Men want different things, including being in a romantic relationship with a soul-mate", etc. If the new statements don't ring true, question them and investigate these thoughts. Try questioning why you wrote "Life is unfair". Is that really true and if you believe it, how does it affect your life? Consider what kind of person you

---

[13] http://www.forbes.com/sites/nancyolson/2016/05/15/three-ways-that-writing-with-a-pen- positively-affects-your-brain/#4d94430b1b93

would be if you didn't believe that statement and then explore the turnarounds.

As for the fears based on actions; these are no more than a call for actions, which you already know. For instance, "If I date this guy, he will break my heart" could be turned around to "What will I do, if he breaks my heart?", or for the next one, "What will I do, if I speak my mind and my boyfriend breaks up with me?" I would also question any assumption, which seems real. Sometimes, the answers are just once google click away. Just notice how your fears might be stopping you from being happy in both the present and potentially, in years to come. I have a fear that this book will be misunderstood or over-criticized, but even more so, that I will fail as a wife and mother, if it transpires that everything I've written is wrong and my husband leaves me.

I am afraid of being laughed at. Does that sound like a good reason to stop writing? Oh yes! But also good enough reason for me to take the necessary simple steps to enable me to carry on!

Questions for self-reflection

Please write down your seven biggest fears regarding relationships, whether you are single or committed. Write "B" next to fears based on belief, and "A" - based on action. Now decide how you will apply the above recommendations You can either change them into positive statements, do the Work on them, use the Emotional Freedom Technique, or write an action plan to minimize the possibility of that fear being realized. Please, consider seeking further help from a therapist, if some fears feel overwhelming. Again, fears should not hold you back from enjoying your life to the full!

1.
2.
3.
4.

5.
6.
7.

When it comes to explaining what fear is to my son, when he turns five years, I will tell him: "Fear is a dream from which you must awaken. Look around you at the kind world and make decisions based on what you see with your eyes, not in your head".

There is one last check required for starting/continuing my project: Do I act out of love or fear? This is a question that I have often encountered in literature but it was only through sessions at Tatyana Latanskaya's Women's Club that I fully understood what it meant. Fear-based decisions only increase fear, whereas in decisions based on love, it is love that multiplies. Jim Carrey, one of my favourite actors, once said: "You can spend your whole life imagining ghosts, worrying about the pathway to the future, but all it will ever be is what's happening here, the decisions that we make in this moment, which are based on either love or fear. So many of us choose our path out of fear disguised as practicality. What we really want seems impossibly out of reach and ridiculous to expect, so we never dare to ask the universe for it.[14]"

Unfortunately, psycho-emotional maturity is something that I see most underdeveloped, even though it is fundamental for marital happiness. I have a dream that this is something that will be taught from kindergarten onwards. When I explain this concept to my son, when he turns five years, I will tell him: "It is your ability to love being with yourself."

Questions for couples:

By what means does he (she) feels most loved?

---

[14]http://www.huffingtonpost.com/2014/05/28/jim-carrey-commencement-maharishi_n_5404156.html

What is the most pleasurable way for you to show your love to him/her?

Do your needs and expectations match one another and if not, could they be combined?

By what means does he (she) like to show his (her) love?

Does that make you feel loved? If not, what would?

PHYSICAL HEALTH

Your body is a garage, where you park your soul.
Wayne W. Dyer

Now that we have learned more about acting out of love and fear, the next important question is: how can I increase my energy level for loving even more maturely?

When I talk about health, it all boils down to energy level. When you have a disease, or are predisposed to ill health (due to poor nutrition, lack of exercise, insufficient sleep or psychosomatic causes), you are expending energy which you could have used more constructively elsewhere. You are more likely to fall into the trap of self-pity and thus, give less love to the world. Why is giving love more important than receiving it?

By giving from your heart, as a natural extension of your kind nature, you receive it in return. Thus taking care of your health becomes a purely a selfish investment in your own happiness and allows you to maximize your potential to love. It is, and should always be, an expression of love for your body; a concept with which many people struggle. I keep on hearing that "If I love my body, I will get lazy and fat", which is exactly the opposite of the truth. As Jessica Ortner says in her book: 'The Tapping Solution for Weight Loss & Body Confidence: A Woman's Guide to Stressing Less, Weighing Less, and Loving More', "it was nearly impossible to take good care of something I hated." If you want long-term results for yourself and your current or future children, or social occupation, loving is essential. Willpower is efficient, but not effective, i.e. it is not enough to ensure long lasting results to your health. Dieting becomes tortuous and exercise, painful and so you quit.

Questions for Self-reflection:

Remember the last time you went to the gym/made a concerted effort to eat more healthily: What was your main motivation? Was it a conscious decision about your physical wellbeing or an emotional response to something else?

For me it was a case of: "I want to take better care of my body today to improve my health for tomorrow. I still have many things that I want to do and so much love to share in the future."

I regard any measure concerning my health as an ongoing investment rather than an isolated, one-off whim. It gives me a feeling of purpose, a sense that my life matters, and that no matter how small my talents, I have something to contribute to the world. Things became noticeably easier after I had read Brian Tracy's 'Psychology of Achievement' and started writing down my goals on a daily basis. I was fueled in my desire to invest in my health, personal development and education. Shortly afterwards, I reduced my meat intake and quit smoking and alcohol. I had goals that were stretching me and that required more energy than I currently had. A renewed interest in my health, coupled with reading Joe Vitale's The Attractor Factor and Key , and working through his The Awakening Course, also helped me to explore toy my disbelieves. Vitale encourages you to toy with your negative believes about yourself. He doesn't advocate that you try to change who you are (which never works) but instead, invites you to look at your potential from a different angle.

I want to take care of my body today so that I can enjoy better health tomorrow. For me it is an investment rather than a one-off choice. It emerged from a feeling of purpose; a sense that my life matters and I can make a contribution to the world, with however seemingly small talents I have.

Before embarking on the next exercise I would like to share a little story that had a strong impact on me. It is drawn from

Jack Canfield's 'Success Principles: How to get from where you are to where you want to be':

A baby elephant is trained at birth to be confined to a very small space. Its trainer secures its leg with a rope to a wooden post planted deep in the ground. This confines the baby elephant to an area determined by the length of the rope and becomes the elephant's comfort zone. Although the baby elephant will initially try to break free, the rope is too strong for the baby elephant to break. It learns that it has to stay in the area defined by the length of the rope. When the elephant grows into a 5-ton colossus that could easily break that same rope, it makes no attempt to do so. It doesn't even try because it learned as a baby that it couldn't break the rope. In this way, the largest elephant can be confined by the puniest little rope. Perhaps you are like that elephant, still trapped in a comfort zone, controlled not by a thin rope and stake but by a set of restrictive beliefs and images that were embedded in you when you were very young. The good news is that unlike the elephant, you can break free and redefine your comfort zone."
There is nothing to stop you, once you know what you want.

Questions for self-reflection

Sit in a very quiet place, where nothing will distract you for half an hour. Answer one question with the help of 10 sub-questions by recording the first thing that comes to mind:

What would you do, if you knew you couldn't fail?

What sphere of work would you choose?

How much money would you be earning?

What type of people would you be associating with?

✍

What global humanity problem would you solve?

✍

What type of sports/physical activity would you engage in?

✍

How many children would you have, if any?

✍

What would you do, if you had more free time?

✍

What charity organization would you open/support and why?

✍

What childhood dream would you realize?

✍

Who would be your mentors?

✍

Again, I hope you felt some discomfort in responding to these questions. I can imagine how much resistance you met from your mind as it started coming up with all kinds of concerns and anxieties about your goals. If nothing like that happened, go back and repeat this exercise! The goals you identify should challenge your perceptions of yourself; otherwise, they are only wishes that will neither increase your energy nor motivate you to achieve more. I would now like you to analyze your answers and find at least one recurring topic amongst them.

What is it?

What do you want to allow yourself to be, to do or to have?

Most of our limits exist only within our imagination and as soon as we take action, tend to dissipate. I still have fears and when they arise, I turn once again turn to the methods described earlier: EFT, the Work of Byron Katie, and writing list of my fears and action plans. My mind always wants to make things more complicated than they are or could be. This way it gets to retain my identity, even when it is inflicting pain. I invite you to notice it, honour it, and start taking action towards your goal as if you were guaranteed to accomplish it. I have been profoundly influenced by books and presentations by Bryan Tracy, Anthony Robbins, and of course, the well renowned Stephen Covey and Napoleon Hill. Each focuses on the importance of long-term thinking and the power of human potential; not by attaching all your happiness to the future, but having worthy goals to strive for and from which to grow and learn.

Once I am clear about what I want to strive for, I become more motivated to take care of my health. Through my decisions and actions I can either prevent or promote a potential chronic disease. According to a report jointly produced by WHO/FAO consultants, entitled 'Diet, Nutrition and the Prevention of Chronic Diseases', chronic diseases are widespread diseases that lay a great burden on society by being the world's most common causes of death. They include: obesity, diabetes, cardiovascular disease, cancer, dental diseases and osteoporosis. Chronic diseases are largely preventable through healthy lifestyles involving a balanced diet and regular physical activity[15]. Rather than dwelling on its terrifying data, I consider the implied recommendations of this report when making decisions and then act out of love.

I keep on asking myself how much my current choice of nutrition/sleep/exercise is likely to affect my long term state of health/energy. I constantly deny myself the gratification of desserts, sleeping in or languishing in front of the TV (apart from 'Game of Thrones'!) It requires the discipline of the famous marshmallow experiment described by Joachim de Posada in his book: Don't Eat the Marshmallow Yet: The Secret to Sweet Success in Work and Life. In several countries, pre-school children were left alone in a room with a marshmallow and told that if they abstained from eating it for 15 minutes, they would receive a second one. Not surprisingly, two thirds of the children could not delay gratification and ate it within one minute. Fifteen years later, the children who managed to wait, were found to have been significantly more successful in both their grades and relationships. They also enjoyed better health. Posada discovered that in Korea, it is common practice for children aged five to be taught the importance of delaying gratification, with a proven, positive impact on the choices they make throughout their lives.

However, since most of us have not had the benefit of such training, we find it hard to resist anything which provides immediate gratification and so struggle with long- term plans.

But the good news is, we're never too old to learn and with dedicated practice over at least 21 days, we can achieve similar results.

As Mykola Latansky, arguably the best motivational speaker in Russian-speaking areas, says in his audio-book, Useful Habits, that the origin of this notion goes back to when NASA astronauts developed a new habit of seeing the world normally despite being upside down. This process of

---

[15] http://www.greenfacts.org/en/diet-nutrition/index.htm#1

adaptation took only 21 days but it took another 21 days for their vision to return to normal once they were able to remain upright.

This led to the claim that any habit can be developed over time but omitted to mention that the success afforded to the astronauts was largely the result of a perfectly controlled environment, free from interference from external factors.

It is therefore far easier to succeed in forming new habits in your lifestyle if you have no distractions. However, since this is rarely the case for most of us, tackling resistance from our minds and bodies to change becomes a little harder.

According to Latansky, the less "visible" to your brain, or the more gradual the shift, in adopting change in your life, the greater your chance of maintaining it. He suggests a gentle approach over a period of around 3 months and never involving more than 3 habits at any one time.

There are thousands of books and guides about healthy lifestyle, offering all kinds of contradictory information. My husband claims that healthy living has become far too 'commercialized' and it's hard to disagree. I leave it up to you to decide which work best for you, so long as they cover three key principles: eat less processed food; spend more time being active, and focus on pursuing a passion. You will then have a reason to get up in the mornings[16]   and enjoy better health.

Questions for self-reflection

What new enjoyable healthy habits/rituals will you develop over the next three months?

---

[16] For more information about this fascinating study on longevity, please visit

www.ted.com/talks/dan_buettner_how_to_live_to_be_100?language=en

I recommend one in physical activity, one in nutrition, and one in daily morning/evening rituals. For instance, in my case these are:

1.   Walking for 20 minutes first thing in the morning, before breakfast or anything else including checking my phone;

2.   Replacing ice-cream with frozen fresh juice or berries;

3.   Thanking my body for my health by doing a five-minute breathing exercise every night before I go to bed.

I emphasize the word enjoyable here. Start off by thinking of some physical activity/habit that you enjoyed in the past. For example, you once tried Pilates and found it appealing, but the instructor was not "your type". Could it be that just a change of teacher would enable you to commit to something you enjoy? Alternatively, why not try something new? What sort of activity appeals to you – a team sport/ Yoga/Zumba/Martial Arts/ Jogging/ Hiking/etc.?

I frequently meet people who have always wanted to dance, but had reservations because of their age or body, or surprise-surprise - childhood traumas. But conversely, there are those often overweight or elderly, who overcame such anxieties and either, joined or founded dance classes. Wouldn't it be fun and worthwhile checking if there's one in your locale or people like you, who could start one?!

Secondly, think of healthy food that you enjoy and would like to add or increase in your diet. This could include fruit and vegetables, foods that contain more fibre, or natural sources of sugars instead of processed sweets and so on. Small changes bring big results.

Thirdly, you could introduce a regular a ritual into your life such a detox involving either full or partial fasting, decreasing your intake of caffeine or meat, or ensuring that you drink two litres of water per day[17].

Even though I invite you to be creative and follow your intuitive sense of pleasure from healthy activities, I would also advise you to consult a reliable specialist prior to starting any new or strenuous activity. It would also be worthwhile seeking guidance from one of the government approved websites on health and exercise. A gentle introduction followed by a gradual increase in activity are key to the prevention of strain or injury to your body and maintain your interest. It is equally important that you monitor changes in your energy levels and level of fitness.

Please remember however, that the person, who knows your body better than anyone, is best, is you! Luise Hay, author of 'You can Heal your Life' and one of the most respected healers in the field of self-help, advocates that we focus our minds on self-love in order to resolve health issues or any other challenges that we are currently facing. In common with many other specialists in this sphere, she believes that all diseases have psychosomatic roots. While full recovery could be a contradictory issue, a combination of psychotherapy with other forms of healing (traditional and non-traditional

---

[17] Nowadays there are numerous mobile applications on nutrition and water intake. I used the "Water control" app. for several months to help me sustain the habit of drinking at least 2 litres each day.

medicine) is an option worth considering. I am currently receiving Gestalt psychotherapy to release energy from emotionally "stuck" places of my soul and this has certainly helped me to progress with this book and get more involved with my profession. I am looking forward to finding psychosomatic roots of my acne, which I have had since I was 13 years old.

Why is physical health important for family life? I made it the second most important part of the chair for a number of reasons. First, it affects you personally, and then by default, your spouses and/or your children. Healthy life can be so much richer than the one plagued by illness yet there are times when we might actually benefit from ill health if it makes us stop and reevaluate what is important in our lives and then instigate profound changes. There is a reason say that if you cannot find time for necessary rest, it will find time for you in the form of disease. I would prefer having a rest in the form of doing what I enjoy, rather than laying down in the hospital bed.

Whether we like it or not, the state of our physical health affects all of the other parts of our maturity chair. The impact of good health or an active investment in our health inevitably results in the following:

- More energy for doing what we enjoy, thus increasing our happiness level;
- A natural inclination to become more loving towards others;
- A greater ability to make others happier, once we have learned how to care of our own happiness;
- An ability to earn more, with less stress or effort
- The development of our brain and level of concentration
- A greater and deeper spiritual connection
- Confidence and pleasure in how we look and project our sex appeal!

And again, after talking extensively about love in respect to health, let's now turn to its opposite – fear. After some doubt,

I have gradually been persuaded by the notion that some people unconsciously "choose" to be ill because they fear self-realization. I personally experienced an underlying fear, when I felt that I was in danger of losing some of my connections with relatives and friends. For me, a perceived fear of success was more a fear of finding myself alone "at the top" and citing disapproval from those closest to me as well as my peers. At the level at which I am currently operating – with my book still to be published – I am perfectly 'safe and sound'. Few people can criticize me. My success or failure has yet to be made public. It's not unlike the time when I kept on postponing my projects because of the acne on my face and feeling overweight. So, in order to move on, I have to ask myself: What would I do, if I were unhindered by this disease of sorts?

Question for self-reflection

Could you be afraid of realizing your immense potential?

I continually remind myself to honour and love my body and improve my health. I am aware that very often, illness is a means by which our bodies demand attention and a desire to be loved and nourished. Knowing this, we should not wait for our bodies to tell us what they need! So, allow me to sum up the concepts discussed in this chapter. Most people take care of their health out of fear of catching one of a million diseases and are thus more focused on avoidance (interpreted by the unconscious mind as illness). But you can choose a more pleasurable option by concentrating on how much good health will contribute to your beautiful machairity, how you will grow as a loving individual and how much more you will be able to give others. Remember: He is rich who gives rather than withholds.

Other specialists offer advice on increasing self-awareness so that you cannot consciously harm yourself; a philosophy close to Buddhist and Sufi teachings. That is why, in order to value yourself, it is so important to get to know yourself and your thoughts.

Finally, when I come to explain the notions covered in this chapter to my son, when he turns five years, I will tell him that physical health is one of the greatest gifts from God. But unlike an inanimate toy, this gift is more like a plant which you and you alone, must nourish daily if you want it to blossom and bear fruit.

Questions for couples:

What physical activities could you and your partner enjoy together?

What types of healthy food are you ready, and conversely not ready, to eat together?

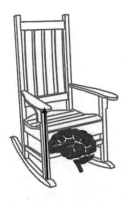

INTELLECTUAL MATURITY

A mind needs books like a sword needs a whetstone.

Tyrion Lannister, 'Game of Thrones' series

I have very special relationships with this chapter because I never thought that this type of maturity would be so powerful in my life. I've always wondered why women barely use the words smart and attractive when defining themselves especially since this is not the case with men. It transpired that for years, I had a problem with the definition of smart, hence my struggle. I saw being intellectual as the degree to which I was able to suppress others with my knowledge: i.e.: as a tool to feeling superior and enhancing my ego, completely divorced from my true nature. Like many of ego's other toys, it was played with subconsciously and separated me from other people (I really wondered why!) So I tried another polarity - being indifferent to any kind of knowledge or skill – to prevent my intellect from scaring people off, especially men. I remember being inspired by the quote: Smart women are those, who can hide their smartness. On both poles, I aimed to make an impression - the knowingly tiring and a dead-end road.

As I became more mindful, I was amazed to observe my desperate attempts to get approval by alternating between showing off and hiding my smartness. By working so hard to make an impression, I am stepping into a dangerous game. I try to guess what type of person someone would most approve of and then fit my behaviour into this illusionary image of my own making. This helps me manipulate them into believing something about me which very often, I am not. As a result, I stray from the only stable ground that I have: self-approval.

By doing the Work, I can begin to identify areas of my behaviour which meet with my approval and as a consequence, find a powerful freedom from my fear of being judged.

I am not saying it's impossible to master the skill of impressing other people, but rather that in the end; it always leaves me feeling empty and lonely. First, I can never be 100% sure that I made the right impression because I simply don't know what people really think about me regardless of what they may say. Secondly, if they appear impressed, I can't help but feel that I have betrayed the real me. In other words, knowing that it is not the real me that has probably impressed them, leads me to believe that I am not all right the way I am. There is also a concurrent fear of being discovered so I keep up an act to maintain that illusionary image of myself. All of this creates tension, which I once tried to relieve with alcohol, tobacco and clubbing and nowadays, with food, internet surfing and oversleeping. Millions of people live with such tension throughout their lives without ever realizing how that vicious circle is the creation of their own, misguided beliefs. I have observed far too many people, and occasionally myself, using intellect in a destructive way that separates them from other people, and most sadly, from their true self. After years of suffering and disconnection I finally grasped a very simple and liberating definition of intellectual maturity:

a continuous process of learning about something that you love to learn and if necessary, share.

Firstly, this new definition includes the word, 'love' which gives it a totally different flavour. It is not a case of 'having to learn' because everybody does, or 'should have learned' because someone else shamed you for it. Because it is based on love, it brings me in closer touch with my true nature. The second key word in my definition is 'continuous' which means that you are ever-developing in a chosen field(s) and relates closely to a concept outlined by Stephen Covey in "Sharpen the [mental] Saw[18]". It may happen that one area will lead you to another or that you switch your areas of interest.

That is fine since any growth will lead to fulfilment and increased satisfaction in both life and your relationships. The happier you are, the more capable you will be in making

---

[18] According to Covey, it means preserving and enhancing the greatest asset you have- YOU- and having a balanced programme of self-renewal in different areas of your life, mentally and physically

others happy. And in that case – your partner and everybody around you will benefit from you sharing your knowledge.

Questions for self-reflection
(Based on The Fifth Practice of The Inner Edge in The 10 Practices of Personal Leadership by Joelle Kristin Jay)

Jay claims that values include the principles, standards, and qualities. She further states, "If you can feel it, see it, or touch it, it is not a value, but an expression of it. A value is the experience behind those things that gives them worth. Here are a few key distinctions: Material goods are not values... People are not values... Goals and activities are not values...

Expectations, aspirations, things, places and even fears can masquerade as values. But values are intangible, not concrete." If you are finding it hard to determine values in your life, it might help to recall something that you are against. For example: I am against drinking alcohol so I value my health. Here is the list of values that Jay gives in her book, please circle 5-7 of them, which resonate with your inner beliefs and write them out:

Abundance   Acceptance   Consistency   Control

Frugality   Fun   Justice   Learning   Relationship Respect

Achievement   Courage   Generosity Love Safety Wisdom

Adventure Courtesy   Gratitude   Loyalty   Service

Security   Authenticity Creativity   Health   Openness

Balance   Discovery   Honesty Order Simplicity Beauty

Excellence   Humor   Peace   Spirituality Choice Family

Faith   Imagination Pleasure Trust Clarity   Independence

Impact   Power   Truth   Compassion   Freedom Wellness

Prosperity   Confidence   Friendship Integrity Quality of life

This will prepare you for further exercises in the following chapters and will help you to answer the next question: based on what you wrote what topics would you enjoy learning the most?

For example, one of my values is health so I would be interested in studying different ways of increasing energy levels in our bodies. Let your mind surf freely right now. At this stage of the exercise, do not think of how and where you would pursue your studies or who would teach you.

Do you remember the scenes in the Matrix film where characters could download any programme into their brains? Any skill or language could simply be attained via a direct download. If you were granted a similar opportunity, what areas of knowledge would you transfer to your brain? Write them down next to your list of values.

Now consider possible ways in which you could gain this desired knowledge through more conventional channels. For example, you could investigate courses run by local organizations or online, or look at private tuition or mentoring schemes.

Finally, decide which 3 out of your 5-7 areas of desired knowledge interest you most and can be studied within the next 12 months. You should now draw up a learning plan by using very simple steps such as making enquiries about enrollment or course content or embarking on study for the entrance exam for a university.

1.

2.

3.

The key is simply getting started and then seeing in practice what you enjoy the most. As Steve Jobs said in his famous Stanford Commencement speech, "you can't connect the dots looking forward; you can only connect them looking backward. So you have to trust that the dots will somehow connect in your future. You have to trust in something — your gut, destiny, life, karma, whatever. This approach has never let me down, and it has made all the difference in my life."

At one point in my life I was obsessed with the idea that learning was a means of achieving my individual goals but now, tend to read more articles and books on family issues and realizing one's potential within marriage. The journey of learning is more important than its destination. Every time I learn something new, it's as if one more light bulb has been switched on in my soul and it is this light which is later reflected in my eyes, speeches and blog posts, as well as how I feel. I love sharing insights from what I have learned and observed and it feels so rejuvenating to regain that curious state of mind of my childhood. It is an interesting blend of childhood playfulness and a mature approach to learning.

At school, we all struggled to attend those obligatory courses in which we had no interest or flair but machairity allows us to choose what we like and grow in it without pressures of time or academic achievement. Small bites of knowledge each day can lead to expertise in our areas of interest in the future. Moreover for me, learning is the golden route to satisfying one of our most basic needs; cited by Anthony Robbins as 'variety'. It is a powerful tool, especially if you are an introvert. So is learning a purely selfish act? To an extent: However, when I learn from other people's research, I am helping them to be useful and the more I learn and understand, the more likely I am to share my knowledge and provide answers to others' problems. This is how both my personal and collective knowledge develop and how learning can become a spiritual process.

Questions for self-reflection

I invite you to study out of love and a desire to give something to yourself and the world. That is why the key question in this chapter is:

How have you come to understand which of your favoured subjects would bring you the most joy?

And I would like to emphasize the word understand, for it presupposes the process rather than the destination, and it also means processing information rather than just collecting factual data.

There is however one secret to developing your intellectual maturity that is absolutely essential – the people you associate with. I first came across this notion in self-development books and found it reiterated by numerous examples from my own and other people's lives. It is much harder to change your old patterns, if you are surrounded by people who are going nowhere: i.e. people who neither have a chair nor are willing to build one; who are just whittling away their time, without any goals or aspirations; who are not serving others in any way. As Latansky says, most people who want to change their lives work so hard on changing themselves that they fail to realize that they need to begin by taking stock of the people who surround them.

When you first make a conscious decision to associate with truth-seekers, motivated intellectual people, ambitious researchers, you might feel uncomfortable, but very soon you will find yourself inspired to learn and grow with them. I know this all too well, because it took me over six years of schooling to realize that once I changed my social environment by cutting off old "friendships" (which were based on fear of loneliness), my grades and volume of reading and learning improved and increased. It was a brave choice to severe old ties but they were quickly replaced by a community more attuned to my aspirations. It was just one girl, who made all the difference in my graduate studies. She introduced me to her intellectual friends and my academic life thrived until I was finally reaching my intellectual potential; something which for years, had been beyond my reach.

Questions for self-reflection

Let us return to Love's opposite: Fear

Have you ever felt afraid of starting something and not being able to finish it? If yes, when?

Have you ever been afraid that your intellectual development will segregate you from your current circle of friends and environment? If yes, when?

Have you ever felt afraid of being regarded as arrogant as a result of your knowledge? If yes, when?

As much as it is important to develop intellectually, it is not the only area of growth. And contrary to popular belief, will not provide answers to all of your questions. There are some things such as unconditional love, compassion and spirituality that exist far beyond the boundaries of intellectual understanding and thus, can be developed only through specific practices and/or associating with certain kinds of people.

If you consider yourself intellectually mature, you have a good foundation for other maturities, and in time, you will attain a deeper understanding of what you love doing and once you have that, an ability to share more, serve more, and connect more.

When I come to explain intellectual maturity to my son, when he turns five years, I will teach him how to ride a bicycle. I will tell him that by mastering this one small skill, he can now go much further and faster and discover the million beauties of this world. Keep on learning!

At this point in my book, I'd like to take the opportunity to credit my husband and his truly contagious reading habit, for inspiring me to read and research much more than I ever thought was possible. Thank you, my love!

Questions for couples:

What are your partner's key interests?

What can you do to best support his/her development of these areas?

How can he/she help you to develop yours?

FINANCIAL MATURITY

Pay your bills, yes. But don't invest in them. Invest in your dreams. What you invest in grows.

Suzette Hinton

When it comes to financial freedom, people usually think that it equates to earning more than they do at the moment. Yet it usually consists of two parts in the following sequence: saving and earning. There is more to it of course, but I have simplified it for the purpose of defining financial maturity as

the ability to earn and sustain a desired income by doing what you love.

Income levels vary dramatically from person to person but the actual sum is far less important than the sense of security it provides. In other words, it is your ability to earn and save enough for your own needs BEFORE you enter into relationship, especially marriage. Why?

1.   Financial management is a skill that does not come automatically to most of us and moreover, is one of the biggest tests in any relationship. Research has shown that the likelihood of divorce decreases as family income rises and to be more specific, Randa Olson (www.randaolson.com), claims that couples with an annual income of $125,000 or more, are half as likely to separate. Although this figure applies to the US it illustrates the importance of financial planning.

2.   It takes more than a marriage contract to guarantee financial security. You must also have the ability to earn, save, and talk to each other about money in a respectful way.

As I see it, it is the part of the chair, without which it cannot stand, let alone rock.

Before we proceed onto how to develop financial maturity, let me talk a little about financial immaturity. Many women, in both the East and the West, choose money over love, built on the premise: "There is no way I can build this part of the chair, so I will choose the easy way". This 'easy' option is firmly attached to the programming we absorb from fairy tales, film, the media and glossy magazines. We are deluded into thinking that all it takes to be a wife of a millionaire is spending his money on looking good for him. We fall into a trap of believing that it is "easy" to wake up next to a man whilst feeling thousands of miles apart or come to terms with the fact that no amount of diamonds or luxurious holidays will ever fill that gap. Again, I am not mutually excluding love and money in a marriage. I am talking about women and men who effectively enter into a form of prostitution, where one is providing his or her services to another person in exchange for material benefits.

I have firsthand experience of this type of situation. I wanted to get married to my ex-boyfriend to fulfil my dream of staying at home. In exchange for his financial and emotional support, I would be a 'good' wife. But in reality, I was evading the fact that my life had no purpose and my lack of self-esteem made me afraid to identify or embrace my passions. I thought that my potential husband would love me forever simply because we were married and I was always by his side. When this man saw this aimlessness in me, he pointed it out several times, but saw no change. And before I knew it, he had broken off our relationship. This was exactly the push I needed to develop myself. So by financial maturity I mean your part of the chair and not your partner's.

Marriage is not an exchange of goods, of whatever value, where you keep track of how much you give and how much you receive in return. It is rather a change towards a better you and perhaps, the best version of you. The more you work on your machairity, the more satisfied you will be with your marriage, regardless of what your partner does or doesn't do. This is especially true when it comes to finance. There are those who continue to believe that it is far simpler to use their partner's chair rather than building that part of their own, but I don't see how this can ever be the easier option. First, you will find yourself imprisoned by the fear of one day losing your partner and /or their money. Secondly, you are imprisoned by the fear that your partner will realize that you are only with them for financial benefits; and thirdly, by an illusion that you can achieve happiness by centering your life on material riches.

Marriage is not an exchange of goods, where you keep track of how much you give and how much you receive in return. It is rather a change towards a better you, perhaps even the best version of you.

Big money is undoubtedly very satisfying and brings with it new experiences, and perhaps even new friends, but alas its allure is too often short-lived. In the background of such pleasure is the hum of anxiety and scarcity. There is no reason why you should not strive for wealth, but it would be insane to make it a priority in your life or make your partner take full responsible for it. We must always be prepared for the unexpected. The wealth of any groom or bride can quickly disappear in the face of illness, an accident, bankruptcy or any other adverse circumstance that life throws at us and there is no amount of insurance that can prevent anything from happening.

The higher you climb, the more likely you are to fall. Indeed, according to Stanley and Danko in The Millionaire Next Door: The Surprising Secrets of American's Wealthy, the average millionaire becomes bankrupt at least 3.5 times. In such cases there has to be safety pillow but in its absence what is a financially dependent spouse to do: Divorce? Sadly, I know people who lived for the sake of material luxuries, and yes - they got divorced at the sight of (temporary!) financial difficulties.

But these situations don't just apply to the traditional model of the man being the main breadwinner. I frequently hear women complaining that they are expected to earn the family income whilst their husbands refuse to work. That is the reason for my questions at the end of this chapter for couples to answer preferably before marriage.

If they have not resolved, or are suffering, difficulties borne from an imbalanced financial responsibility I always ask:

1.   What does it mean to you? Because it is barely about a particular event but rather, the related beliefs which prevent effective communication about how the situation could be addressed and resolved.

2.   How did you co-create this situation? A man's decision not to work or contribute to the family income cannot be excused by the fact that his wife happens to love her job and is happy to provide for them financially. This is usually the result of a pattern of behaviour which must be identified if they are to reach a happier state.

I would like to underline once again that it does not matter how much you earn or save, but that you have the skill of bringing it to the level of self-sufficiency. Gone are the days (until the end of the 19th century) when the majority of women could enter professional occupations because of their gender, or indeed, were not expected to work. Nowadays, despite the continued existence of a gender pay gap, women throughout the world are able to earn their own living from jobs they enjoy. But the path to finding such work is not always easy or straightforward. In my case, I had to work in a variety of jobs in six different countries before I found the one that I love and now earn from. I also had to struggle with poverty for a long time before I learned to develop the necessary mindset for earning enough to live on and from thereon in, learned how to save, invest and spend more healthily. On the way, to maintain my skills, I am studying the Platinum Group of Mykola Latansky, to develop the abundance mindset and to surround myself with people who have similar goals. And more recently, I am finding inspiration in Sophia Amoruso's #Girlboss on how despite patriarchal obstacles, a woman can and should be striving to do what she loves and earn from it.

I would also recommend related texts by Joe Vitale, Jack Canfield, Harv Ecker, Anthony Robbins, Bryan Tracy and Vadim Zeland which encompass the following points of advice:

- Discipline yourself to save a specific amount
- Always work as effectively as possible
- Follow your passion
- Share your wealth with those in greater need
- Adopt an attractive personality
- Overcome your fears/ beliefs about money and understand that these are a choice and can therefore be changed
- Shift your focus from money to serving people,
- Learn how to perceive money-making as a spiritual activity,
- Be grateful for whatever you have right now,
- Keep up to date with modern technologies and trends[19].

The methods for achieving the above vary from author to author and you should choose one which suits you best. I found it very helpful to listen to Bill Harris's interview with the world's greatest teachers[20]. You will immediately get a glimpse of their language and whether it appeals to you. There are many videos available on YouTube which recommend other teachers. You might also find inspiration in films such as The Secret, The Opus, Butterfly Circus, etc. while Brandon Boshnack on the Intuitive Meaning website recommends a further list of similar movies[21] including:

---

[19] For example, by following mobile applications released in their thousands every day

[20] https://www.centerpointe.com/teachers/

[21] http://intuitivemeaning.com/2010/04/top-5-inspirational-movies-like-the-secret/

Beyond the Secret, The Secret Behind The Secret, The Compass, The Shift and Thoughts Become Things.

As Jack Canfield says in his books, there is no magic to it. It's a simple law of probability: the more you read/watch different authors; the more likely you are to find an influential teacher. Similarly, the more seminars you attend on financial freedom, the more information you will accrue to help transform your situation. Nowadays, there are more possibilities than ever for us to directly access presentations by internationally renowned specialists, as shown by Bryan Tracy coming to Kyrgyzstan, my home country, for a one-day seminar in April 2015.

There is no reason, either financially or mentally, for not starting straight away.

In his audio book, Useful Habits, Latansky claims that most people's perception of success follows a common sequence: wealth >happiness >health. They think that only when they have a certain amount of money, will they be able to relax and be happy, and when they have both time and money, they will be able to care for their health. They are therefore prepared to do a job they hate, work with discouraging and negative people, and compromise their relationships to reach that point. In the eyes of society, they might appear successful but only externally. When you talk to these people, or live with them, you sense a permanent dissatisfaction which could have been prevented. We then begin to understand that for long term results, the most highly effective people follow a different sequence: happiness>health>wealth. They are employed in jobs that they love, find enjoyment in their work even if it involves long hours, continually look after their health and as a result attain material riches. Wealth becomes a natural consequence rather than a starting point or as Napoleon Hill says, "you get fulfilment from your work that money cannot buy". When you do not feel threatened by not having something, you are much more likely to achieve it.

Questions for self-reflection

Please turn back to the previous exercises: What are my Values and What do I love doing. Now rewrite the seven values and the correlating activities next to them, if they fall into the 'value' category. If not, enter them in the 'other' column. Next to each activity, write how you could be earning money from it.

For example, my value is 'impact' and its related activity is hosting public events. I could earn money from this activity by charging a fee as a host. Again, allow yourself to think freely, without concerns and limitations. I advise you to have at least seven activities in the list.

Values   Activities   How to make money out of it?

Please circle 2 or 3 activities that you could begin immediately, with reference to your current levels of education and work/life experience and write 'now' next to them.

Then circle the 2 or 3 activities that would require more preparation and further study/ knowledge and write 'more' next to them.

Finally, please circle 2 or 3 activities that you would enjoy doing the most, even if you were not paid, and mark each 'true'.

The chances are that activities which you marked as 'true' are the most reliable and most accurate in terms of finding a means of earning money.

Now that we've had a glimpse into how to make money, we can look at how we can make it our friend. It's actually no different to how we make friends with people; by serving each other without any expectations. But how can you serve money? This can be done in a variety of ways: When you invest it well or when you prevent it from getting into trouble by not overspending; or by keeping it away from those who use it to make themselves look like someone they're not. Money, like people, thrives on self-investment and in an age of ever-sophisticating technology, the only way to stay in the market is through continuous professional development.

 In one of his speeches, Latansky quotes Bill Gates, who has advised that anyone who earns less than $100,000 a year should invest in their education[22]. As in any investment, there is bound to be a return and in the case of education, this is your financial and professional growth,

Questions for self-reflection

Again let's turn to our fears. Take a deep look at yourself and ask:

Am I scared that money will make me a worse person? Does money have that power?

Am I afraid of people asking for money and being unable to refuse them?

---

[22] https://www.gobankingrates.com/personal-finance/6- things-bill-gates-says-should-money/

Am I scared that an elevated financial status would put my friendships at risk?

What other negative beliefs do I have around money? And are they valid?

Listening to Jack Canfield's *Self-Esteem and Peak Performance*, I was struck by one question in particular: "Does money make you a better or worse person?" and when I passed it on to my students, I kept on hearing the same answer : "It makes you worse, especially children!" But Canfield would argue that in reality, money or its related power only "amplifies who you already are". If you were a jerk before, you will become a bigger jerk after becoming rich. That is why it is so crucial to work on our character before we become financially mature. There are many more myths about money that we keep on believing simply because we have never actually examined them. Financial management is not taught as a general subject at school and so we lack a basic knowledge of how to accumulate money or how to become friends with it.

Left to our own resources, we usually learn about finance through trial and error when we are single, and through endless battles when we are married. It is therefore crucial that we educate ourselves in this sphere as early as possible.

I often encounter beautiful, well-educated and financially secure women who find themselves unable to enter into a meaningful relationship. Their common complaint is that men are put off by the fact that they don't need a man to provide them with anything material. Their financial position would be ideal if they were entering into a business transaction and as we have already discussed, needing something from someone else is not a good foundation for any relationship. However, just because there are too many women seeking financial stability in men, it doesn't automatically mean that those who are not have sufficient grounds for a loving relationship. That is why I am talking about the entire chair, not just a leg of the chair. I invite you to take a closer look at the power of money and see how it reverberates across every aspect of the chair enabling you to attain the following:

- Pay for books/courses/consultations with gurus of psycho-emotional development;
- Cover the costs of beneficial and enjoyable physical activities and healthy food;
- Pay for the courses/books/training/internships in areas of intellectual interest;
- Help your friends and strangers invest in themselves, attend different social events/interest groups;
- Serve humanity with your resources by supporting people less fortunate than you;
- Cover the costs of maintaining your appearance: cosmetics/clothes/ spiritual healer.

When I come to explain financial matters to my son, when he turns five years, I will tell him: "Sweetheart, money is meant to help you be a better, kinder person. You can earn it by doing what you love." And I will talk about the marshmallow principle, described earlier. We will conduct this experiment again and again, with explanation, feedback and support until he learns the importance of delaying the gratification.

Questions for couples:

The following questions are taken from the book: 'First Comes Love Then Comes Money: a Couple's Guide to Financial

Communication', by Bethany and Scott Palmer[23]. They advocate that couples cannot afford NOT to find answers to the following questions:

Which do you think is most appropriate in marriage: a joint or separate bank account?

How did your parents spend money?

How did your parents save money?

Will we be a dual income family, or will one of us stay at home with the children?

Do you think paying bills should be done separately or together?

Are you saver or spender? Do you seek risks or security?

Do you currently work within a budget?

Are you conservative or aggressive in your investment?

---

[23] Questions drawn Forbes magazine: *20 Crucial Questions to Ask Before Saying "I Do"*, https://www.forbes.com/pictures/hgme45ekd/the-money-talk/#1f89a5a57897

What are your income goals?

✍

Should we consider entering into a prenuptial agreement?

✍

Have you ever lost a large amount of money in investments?

✍

Do you want to rent or your own home?

✍

What mistakes have you made with money?

✍

What is the most expensive item you have ever purchased?

✍

What cause you stress, when it comes to money?

✍

Did your parents ever talk about money?

✍

Do you track your savings and spending?

✍

Do you subscribe to an employer retirement plan?

✍

How important is planning for retirement for you?

✍

Do you give to charitable organizations?

It may sound awkward, or extremely uncomfortable to talk about this subject, but believe me, it is worthwhile. I am continually confronted by male clients who come out with the same old rhetoric: 'we got divorced because after a while, what I earned was not enough for this b*tch.' The immediate reaction is adverse judgment of the woman and sympathy for her poor husband but only until you realize that the situation could have been avoided if together, they had discussed money before they married. Always remember that your marital happiness far outweighs any discomfort arising from questions and discussion about money.

SOCIAL MATURITY

If a person loves only one other person and is indifferent to all others, his love is not love but a symbiotic attachment, or an enlarged egotism.

Erich Fromm

It was my original intention to centre this chapter on the necessity to be friendly towards people around us including of course, your partner, his/her relatives and friends and in particular, your in-laws. I like to joke that the word "husband" contains - band –which if interpreted as a band of his relatives and friends, means that a woman marries a whole host of people! If she is unable or willing to make friends with them, it is all too likely that she will be doomed to an unhappy marriage. The reverse is also true since the word 'wife' is an abbreviation for "wires of infinite family everywhere".

But after reading Erich Fromm and Eckhart Tolle, it occurred to me that social maturity involves much more than just being friendly and **is actually about loving everyone around you to lesser or greater degrees**. Can this even be possible? Could it be that many of us are too afraid to extend our love to our neighbours? Or fear love because we associate it with something hurtful or potentially dangerous?

I observe many people confusing love with being obedient and/or passive and many will tell me: "If I love people too much, they will use me." My response to them is that it is not love that you're dealing with but rather, your need for approval, your escape from your perceived loneliness, your unspoken (and therefore unfair) expectations of trading in kindness, your actions born from fear that you will lose someone's love. None of the above has anything to do with love. You can still say "no" or even oppose violence if necessary, in a loving way - without hurting yourself. The gift and receipt of love will always bring far more joy than any other sort of present.

That may sound like some vision of Utopia in an age of consumerism but I hope that this chapter will encourage you to appreciate how it could well become our new reality.

As Fromm says, for far too many of us, the most important aspect of love is in receiving rather than giving. We have been programmed to believe that ultimately, it is love which will make us happy, save us from loneliness, and become winners in life. We should therefore do everything in our power to get it. In reality, however, love is a state of mind which we can only connect to by working on ourselves. It is as much an intrinsic part of us as our vital organs. So there is no point in searching for it elsewhere. It can't be replaced by something else and why try to implant something that we already have?

Love is apparently the only thing that matters at the end (?) of our earthly life. In his research, the father of near-death experience, Raymond Moody M.D. interviewed thousands of people who had been pronounced clinically dead for several minutes before regaining consciousness. Many of them reported experiencing similar sensations: they described travelling through a tunnel towards radiant light, and how they had a panoramic view of their lives permeated with small acts of kindness. In the study they were asked two questions: "How have you expanded your capacity to love? What wisdom have you gained from your experience?"

For me these questions seem just as relevant to anyone embarking on a relationship for in a sense, marriage is that kind of transcendental moment of truth, or the beginning of a new life. These questions represent the two most important skills that we should develop before entering into marriage, if we wish to ensure happiness.

Questions for self-reflection

How would you answer these two questions right now?

How have you expanded your capacity to love?

What wisdom have you gained from your experience?

_____

Interestingly, the thousands of people whom Moody studied were not asked about their love for their spouse, how successful they had been in their careers or the countries that they have visited. They weren't even asked about their charitable acts or the number of times they prayed. They were simply asked about their overall capacity to love. And I think the second question is strongly related to the first - [by developing love] how have you become wiser? If I had a similar experience, I would ask the angels: Where do I get begin, if I want to expand my capacity to love to the full? Could it be the stillness within me or in a deep internal space yet to be discovered?

When I still myself, I see just how many judgements I have formed against people, especially those with whom I spend most of my time. And so I've judge them freely and mercilessly, on Byron Katie's 'Judge- Your-Neighbour' worksheet. You may be surprised to hear that it brought a sense of relief to learn that prior to loving them; I passed judgement on each one.

The first 'neighbours' I judged were none other than my parents, for during my formative years, it is they who informed my story more than anyone else. In the past, I saw myself as an unhappy victim in our relationship and this prevented me from expanding my capacity to love them. I thought I could escape all of that and form a happy marriage with "someone less cruel than my parents". But how could that possibly happen if in my mind, I believed myself unlovable because allegedly my parents didn't love me? Naturally, this impacted on my relationships with other people. When I became aware of this deeply rooted perception, around which I had formed my identity, I questioned it, and discovered an unknown sense of freedom and lightness. It was as though a backpack filled with heavy rocks had finally fallen from my shoulders. The sense of inner peace was so overwhelming that I cried for three hours solid!

Questions for self-reflection

It is now time for you to review your first intimate relationship; that which you had with your parents.

Are you satisfied with this relationship?

Has it led to continued feelings of resentment or guilt? If so, what are they?

How will you deal with the situation?

To whom will you turn for help to resolve it?

It was also a revelation to discover that in order to connect to my parents and anybody else for that matter, I do not need them to be enlightened, wise, and loving. In fact, it transpired that those who I believe inspire the least love in me are my best teachers with regard to my spirituality. I therefore decided to start with them and then, think about how I relate to strangers. I found that my inability to love the rest of the world is an indicator of how much I can truly love my spouse. So all I need to do is find a place within me which allows me to love towards everyone, but to different degrees. Hence, if I was single, I wouldn't bother trying to find 'the one', who like Santa Claus, is a fantasy figure on whom you have projected a specific role, usually within a set timeframe. As you get to know people better, you begin to see less attractive sides of their character that jar with how you pictured them and disappoint you.

Believing in the existence of 'the one' or 'a best friend' is like believing in Santa Claus - somebody has to play this role for you...

I have noticed that whenever I use my marriage as a shelter from the hostilities of the outside world, both my anxiety and fear of losing my partner's love increase. I therefore try to compensate by doing things to please him, often to the cost to my own integrity, and I feel separated from other people and a need to defend myself from them. Worse, I bring that unresolved hostility into my family. I fully expect my partner to comfort me, only to find that this is not always possible. He should not be expected to comfort me, regardless of whether he is a world famous psychotherapist, because quite simply, that is my job.

So what role does the outside world play in my life? It allows me to connect more strongly with my inner world and awakens and stimulates my consciousness of everything around me. When striving to connect with others, I am not seeking happiness but rather, as Tolle says, a greater level of consciousness, beyond the dichotomies of 'good and bad' or 'happiness and misery'. In this state, I cannot help but love other people and want to share things with them, and that's an exciting enough project for any lifetime.

I strive to give rather than receive. According to Fromm, many of us confuse giving with sacrificing something. They think that by giving, they will lose something whereas in my experience, giving equates with receiving. As my mentality shifts from victimized "beggar" to an abundant giver, I find myself filled with renewed strength and inspiration. If I fill and then seal a barrel with water, it will soon become too stale to support any form of life but if I regularly release and replenish the water, I will maintain its purity.

The ability to give in relationships is essential and I have identified five areas which I find the most fulfilling:

1.   For-giving
2.   Being genuine
3.   Listening to what people are saying and heightening your awareness of how they are feeling
4.   Sharing your talents and knowledge
5.   Choosing discomfort as a means of reaching a more comfortable zone.

1. The first act of giving is for-giving. As my long-term relationship with this word shows, all it actually means is giving up my victim story and moving forward. In other words, it's about finding an alternative interpretation of an event, beyond my ego. One of my most liberating experiences from going through Byron Katie's Work, was forgiving my mother for her words. I had long regretted holding grudge against her but there was nothing I could do because my ego was determined to protect my identity as a victim. My feeling bitter resentment of my mother's rhetoric towards my acts of disobedience lasted for years and I continually told people that I had been verbally abused as a child. It was only by questioning this issue with the Work that I was able to see the bigger picture. I then realized that just like me, my mother was an innocent being but one whose actions were fueled by her belief that I was an extremely difficult child whom she found difficult to handle. There were neither victims nor perpetrators; just two confused people. No words or actions regarding forgiveness could ever restore my internal balance and I had to open my mind to resolve that long running drama. So yes, I did have to give something –my time and attention – to gain the power to love her again. The effect was multiplied when I myself became a mother of my child.

Anyone who has studied psychology will have come across the notion that the way in which parents rear their children influences their lives well into adulthood. But I had become entrapped by the belief that my parents were to blame for whatever misfortunes befell me, from low self-esteem and under-achievement to meaningless relationships, and even my acne. And it all seemed highly plausible until I stopped to question it and finally acknowledged that there was nothing I had to forgive them for. The result was a sense of indescribable freedom. Everyone, including you my reader, is a beautiful, innocent human being who from time to time, happens to act in accordance to misguided beliefs but you will only appreciate why, when you remove your ego from the centre stage of your story.

Questions for self-reflection

We hear more and more about the benefits of forgiving, and yet we don't always know how to go about it. I created the following exercise at a period when I felt overwhelmed by resentment that I had been carrying for years. It helped me to let go, on both a physical and metaphysical level.

-        On a separate paper make a list of people to whom you have felt attracted, but who you think have hurt you in some way or another. For example: someone promised to call you but never did, or your partner broke off with you in the cruelest way imaginable. Please don't berate yourself for harbouring any resentment. In fact the longer the list, the better since it means that you are becoming more conscious of your innermost feelings. At the beginning, my list contained 54 people!

 Now imagine that they are all in waist-deep in a swamp (of your soul), calling for your help. They are all waiting for you to first take notice of them and then help them (and yourself). Imagine you are on the bank and able to help them (and yourself) by offering your hand. Before you save anyone, you will say things to them based on the answers to the following questions:

-        What exactly has she/he done to you? Feel free to give full vent to your feelings here since there is barely anything more destructive than suppressed anger. Now is the time to let them know!

-        What has his/her hurtful act taught you? If nothing comes up, be still and wait till the answer finds you.

-        What was your part in co-creating this situation? In other words, to what degree were you not a complete victim?

After you have addressed each one, the swamp will disappear in a massive surge of gratitude. However, nothing will grow in soil which lacks nutrients, so we must fertilize our former swamp with potash   or heartfelt love. Only then, will you be able to regenerate growth in your former swamp and with time, it will flower with positive affirmations such as: 'People treat me kindly'; 'I deserve to be cared for'; 'I am surrounded by kind people', etc.

Breathe! I hope you feel better! And get ready for good things to appear unexpectedly!

Another powerful method of coping with forgiveness is the previously mentioned Emotional Freedom Technique (Tapping). There are various videos available on the internet to suit different people but for a more powerful experience which you conduct yourself, I recommend attending the annual, online World Tapping Summit. From a personal perspective, I found that tapping exposes many hidden grievances and has led me to forgive all manner of things, including a seemingly incidental occasion when my father didn't hug me when I really wanted it.

It is a magical tool, which I believe should be taught in Primary schools so that children learn how to release their inner tensions from an early age. In his book, The Tapping Solution for Pain Relief, Nick Ortner cites recent research which proves that lower back pain is related to suppressed resentment. Thus, the more we work on letting go, the better we become in managing pain, especially muscular which is hard to treat with medicines. It certainly works for me and I waved goodbye to chronic menstrual pain simply by tapping on resentment which I had piled up against my unsupportive professors. So why not give it a try?

Let's get acquainted with another method - Radical Forgiveness – which I learnt in classes at Tatyana Latanska's Women's Club and which is outlined on the website : www.radicalforgiveness.com . Its founder, Colin Tipping, claims that forgiveness is the key to manifesting miracles in your life, and a method which has "helped thousands of people release toxic pain from old emotional wounds, free themselves from harmful behaviour patterns and experience deeper levels of self-acceptance than they've ever known before." Tipping has written numerous books on the topic and has free and paid on-line tools. I filled out the Radical Self-Forgiveness/Acceptance Worksheet, which is available in his website for free. For this exercise I worked on my own history of "cheap" behaviour and was excited to feel a reconnection with myself! I especially liked the strong statements towards the end, which undoubtedly provided me with peace of mind.

2   The second act of giving that I suggest is the gift of being able to pronounce a genuine "yes" or "no." This response should be drawn from a deeply peaceful state of mind, or as Tolle would say: "one that does not bring further suffering". Any reader of philosophy will be familiar with the importance of being able to say 'no' for the sake of your integrity and especially, attaining your goals. While you might agree that this is desirable and respect those who are able to stay true to themselves, it's still a hard thing to do and in the beginning, feels extremely uncomfortable.

There is a little mantra by Jack Canfield that I find particularly helpful: "I am comfortable feeling uncomfortable". I repeat it to myself whenever I feel anxious in a new environment, or especially in the company of successful people. It is something that I'm still working on, alongside authenticity and how I can represent my true self. Looking to re-learn this skill which fades as we grow up; I found three effective methods: the Work, the Screamfree formula, and the 8-step formula of Shari Harley[24].

For the Work to work, all you have to do is complete the statement: "If I say 'No' to my boss/employer/mother/best friend, they will " and then explore whatever you wrote with four further questions, followed by turnarounds. You might be amazed how funny some of your beliefs about saying 'no' sound! I am not saying it is easy, but there are certain ways in which you can over-ride any hesitancy you may have. Harley suggests that expressing your true feelings and giving honest feedback is much easier if it's something you've agreed on at the start of a relationship. For example: My colleague constantly turns up late for meetings but even though this annoys me, I still feel uncomfortable about saying 'no' whenever she asks me to wait for her. Unsurprisingly, this causes me to build a wall of inner resentment against her, alongside anger at myself for not speaking up. However, had we sat down and discussed the issue from the outset, with each explaining our points of view (no matter how awkward) I would have felt far more comfortable in simply telling her "Please do not arrive late at these meetings". The truth is that whilst that would not guarantee any change in my colleague's behaviour, it would have given me peace of mind, and that's all I have control over. And the next time it happened, I would have felt more empowered to say 'no'. The same applies to any relationship: If boundaries are agreed at the beginning, you free yourself from accumulating unnecessary stress.

There are numerous reasons why groups, companies, and couples fall apart but somewhere along the line, there is usually a breakdown in communication. One of the greatest answers on how to give a genuine 'yes' or 'no' is provided by Hal and Jenny Runkel in their books: Screamfree Marriage: Calming Down, Growing Up, and Getting Closer and

---

[24] http://candidculture.com/wp-content/uploads/2012/12/Eight-Steps-to-Say- Anything-to-Anyone-in-Two-Minutes-or-Fewer-by-Shari-Harley.pdf

Screamfree Parenting: The Revolutionary Approach to Raising Your Kids by Keeping Your Cool . They employ a simple formula: "Calm Down. Grow Up. Get Closer."

 - *Calm down* - by leaving the room for a moment to prevent yourself from responding impulsively to a situation. This will allow you speak and act in a more conscious manner; the first thing that people lack before or during a conflict.

- *Grow Up* - by understanding your own pattern or role in the conflict. No matter how unfair the other person appears at the moment, it is the result of some action by you. A lot of maturity is required if you are to admit this. Runkel says that people have problematic patterns rather than problems and should "Simply. Stop. Dancing. And then take a different dance step." Once you admit your share, you have enough to resolve the whole situation.

- *Get Closer* – After you were able to take a break, realise your own pattern, you are now ready to approach your partner, genuinely admit your wrong and ask for what you would like to receive without getting attached to the answer. The Runkels call this Authentic Self-representation; something that couples avoid at all cost because of the perceived risk.

Let's revisit the case of the late colleague. You calm down by saying "If you could excuse me for a moment", when the person comes. You realize that she makes no attempt to arrive on time because you shouted at her or made a sarcastic comment instead of giving a direct message. So the next step would be to 'lay your cards on the table' by telling her that you know how you created this situation, how you feel about it, and what you would like to request of her. For instance, you could say that you feel upset about having to wait for her that it undermines your authority. You could then say that you realize you neglected your responsibility by not emphasizing the need for punctuality and gently ask your colleague to arrive on time in the future. Again, there are no any guarantees about the reaction from the other side, but at least you will be at peace with yourself, and that's all you are in charge of.

I've noticed that the more I practice presenting my authentic self, the easier it becomes; rather like exercising a muscle. I then begin to notice that I expect less from other people. I accept them for who they are simply because I have learned to give myself love and be loyal to my true self. And we all adore loyalty!

Presenting this gift to the world does not guarantee me many friends (especially in the beginning), but I know that those who stay within my sphere, appreciate the real me. It all starts with a decision to take risks without any guarantees. There is always a chance that particular people will never accept that authentic part of me. But why would that matter if I no longer have a need for the external approval?!

3. The third gift that I encourage everyone to give for their own sake is listening - noticing people, discovering who they are without automatically applying your story on them. It is perhaps one of the craftiest and rarest gifts you can make; and yet it is the most valuable one. This one skill alone is already transforming my more complicated relationships. When my friend or a stranger is speaking, I work on noticing my inner dialogue. I strive to be there for her/him without needing to know or analyze what they're saying. All I need to do is listen and in so doing, ensure that they are listening to themselves. I am more attuned to her/his emotional state, and this encourages me to find the correct way to respond to how they are feeling by offering advice, words of comfort, casual chat or good humour etc. I have always wanted a friend who truly understood me and when become that kind of friend to myself, I am able to be a similar friend to others.

4. Sharing your skills, talents and knowledge is something I have talked about in the previous chapters. I believe that everyone has something of unique value to give to the world, and it's only a matter of trial and error, as well as asking the

right questions, to discover what that might be. In most religions, believers are expected to share their wealth and some religious scholars have expanded the definition of this concept to include skills and talents alongside material possessions.

5. Giving comfort to the here and now means consciously choosing gentle discomfort. It is something advocated by the majority of motivational speakers. How do I give relinquish my comfort zone? We must first understand that if we always do what we've always done, we'll always get what we've always got. And secondly, we must understand the importance of making any transition, a smooth process by changing one habit or pattern of behaviour at a time. A common indicator of comfortable behavior is the avoidance of potential conflict by portraying yourself as the kind of person someone else would approve of. Comfort is also found in avoiding any criticism or rejection by lying low and being inconspicuous. So, in order to avoid such entrapment, we must consciously open ourselves up to new outcomes, new possibilities, and new depths of friendship. It's only by releasing ourselves from the shackles pseudo-comfort, that we will ever gain integrity and authentic relationships.

When I come to explain these concepts to my son, when he turns five years, I will tell him that social maturity is learning to love people for what they are. It is not just about seeing "good" things in everything and everybody. It is looking at them in a mirror, not through a spyglass. I will definitely read him Byron Katie's book for little children Tiger-Tiger, Is it True? I will tell him how easy it is to love people, when we question what we think. I will also tell him about The Gingerbread Man who ended up nowhere by avoiding social connection with any of the forest's other inhabitants and by employing the same technique on each one of them.

88

Questions for couples:

Would you consider your partner your best friend? Would
he/she consider you as his/her best friend?

Who are your partner's close friends? Have you met with
them? What is your impression of them? Please share your
views with your partner.

How often do you and your partner meet up with your friends,
either on your own or together? How comfortable are you
spending time together, in the company of these friends?

What is your impression of your partner's family? How often
do you visit /socialize with them? Are you both comfortable
with the amount of time spent with them? (I highly
recommend "Fire of in-laws" from Screamfree marriage for
deeper understanding of the importance of the topic.)

Finally, what conflicts did you have before you married?

The truth is that these conflicts will most likely intensify with
marriage. How do you feel about that?

Are you ready to address this issue?

SPIRITUAL MATURITY

You are not the drop in the
ocean, but the ocean in a drop.
                    Rumi

I remember reading in *Seven Habits of Highly Effective People* by Stephen Covey that you should "not just tolerate, but celebrate differences." It was like a big punch in my Ego's face: "Why would I celebrate my honey's bad habits?!" And what looked like a nice idea seemed better suited to saints, or people like Covey himself. The separation of labels such as good (me) and bad (others), enlightened (teachers) and too complicated (me) seemed very real for a time for it served as a good reason to stick to my story and stay in my comfort zone. I didn't ask these thoughts to dissolve but instead, asked myself, "Can I approach things differently? What if I were able to love my sweetheart unconditionally? What if I could actually appreciate what I considered to be his flaws?"

My immediate response was: "Okay, but give me a reason why we should celebrate differences in our spouses' characteristics?" Well, in yaprak sarmasi, that delicious Turkish starter, you don't expect the rice to taste the same as the marinated vine leaves and indeed, appreciate that it is the combination of complementary ingredients that gives the dish its unique flavour. You never stop to consider which individual flavour tastes best.

In yaprak sarmasi, a delicious Turkish starter, you don't get upset that rice tastes different to marinated vine leaves but rather, appreciate that the recipe's unique comes from a perfect combination of different ingredients.

Likewise, if differences in character are acknowledged and valued, partners find themselves connected to each other and the world around them on a more meaningful level: one that cannot be attained through the human mind or logic, described by words. It is purely spiritual.

The point of this chapter is not to talk about religion, but spirituality. The concepts are related, but do not mean the

same thing. "Spiritual", according to Marriam-Webster dictionary means, 'concerned with religious values'. Thus, spiritual maturity in the context of our topic is
following religious values in order to see and love universal wisdom.

It is a strong sense of knowing that you are connected to, and are part of, something far greater than the confines of your human body and experience. In my understanding, spirituality is viewing the world through your spirit, not your mind. It is a separate dimension. And for me the difference lies between living in a two- dimensional or three-dimensional world. Consider the following analogy. Cockroaches live in a two-dimensional world. If you put a piece of food on the floor and pull it away, they will follow it. But as soon as you elevate it, they are unable to see it unless they scale the wall. This doesn't mean that they are unaware of what is going on above them since after all, they will scurry away from something descending from above. It's more a case of their being able to grasp a projection of the moving object on the floor. Similarly, some of us stay within the cockroach mindset, without realizing that we can develop a much richer perception of the reality. What seems to us like a terrifying dark shadow (and most volumetric objects are seen as shadows on the plane) is in fact a harmless, plush teddy bear, if we look at it from a 3D perspective. The two dimensions in the case of humans are: the past and the future. Many of us interact with our partners on the basis of usually negative memories and not necessarily positive expectations based on these memories. But when we view our partner, or anything else for that matter, from the third dimension or in the present, we have no trouble celebrating our differences. We still use the past and future for practical purposes, but not to define ourselves or our partner.

The two dimensions in the case of humans are: the past and the future. Many of us interact with

our partners on the basis of usually negative memories and not necessarily positive expectations based on these memories.

It becomes much easier to forgive, accept and even love our differences. As a result, our disagreements begin to unfold in a quite different fashion. Something what caused us pain is enlightening and brings us closer together. Seeing the world in 3D, doesn't mean that I'll suddenly be surrounded by only plush teddy bears, but rather, when an angry grizzly approaches, I'll see it for what it is and then take flight, fight or stand my ground. Instead of relying on guesswork, I'll be equipped to ask and listen (remember the gift of attentive listening?). I WILL see things more fully and thus make kinder and wiser decisions.

As I said earlier, it is essential to go beyond the two-dimensional paradigm, when it comes to truly fulfilling relationships. That is why I have chosen to use a chair as a metaphor for 3- dimensional living. It is a solid, multi-facetted object that offers you the greatest support at the end of a long day. Yet some people never choose to 'build' it. It is of course, possible to live without it, since just like cockroaches; we are physically able to survive on a certain level. Nevertheless, any prominent family psychologist will tell you that the one thing that many couples lack, which could drastically improve their relationships, is spirituality: something far beyond bodily and worldly experience.

Another exercise that I recently came up with is called the chair. It also helps me enormously to give my husband and myself spiritual love. In my understanding, the spiritual love is the love that we receive from the Universe, God, Allah, Buddah, or however you name it. The more we are able to give it to our partners, the more spiritually mature we become. And as we saw from the above paragraph, it does not require that much of a big effort – just the awareness and the chair. If you are standing, please sit down on a chair. Close your eyes

for 20 seconds and remember someone you had a
disagreement with – recently or long time ago. What did this
person say to you? What did he or she do to you?

Now take a deep breath and feel your chair. Touch the
handles, feel the seat, the upper part of the chair with your
back. Get up. And mentally put this person on this chair. Sit
back on the chair not as you, but as the person you had a
disagreement with.

Let's see, I can remember my husband who threw his socks on
the floor. I see he is tired after long working day, and he is
hurt from my tone of the voice. Oh, if I was him, I wouldn't
want to pick up my socks. I see the pattern. The point here is
not to do the guess game of how the person felt, but to shift
the focus from yourself to this person.

In your situation, what does this person feel in the moment?

What does this person see?

Why is this person acting this way?

How does he or she see you in the moment of your
disagreement?

Now please open your eyes.

Did you feel like you understood this person a little bit more?

Did you start liking this person more?

Understanding brings love. You cannot hate a person, when
you truly understand him. The more you understand, the
more you fall in love without wanting to get something from
this person. My freedom and love are one chair away. And
chair is good news for me, for I tried other methods and they
didn't quite work for me. For me, such expression as putting
yourself on someone's place is too abstract, so I tried to be
more literal, like wearing someone's shoes - it didn't bring
good results, for they can be too small or too big, and they

smell sometimes. Chair is the most available tool anywhere. Every place has a chair. When I go to a desert or open space, I can carry a folding chair with me, just in case, if I hate someone. I can use it anywhere, and it takes me just a couple of seconds to find it and several minutes to do the exercise.

And you can use this little secret chair during or after fight. But don't use it before a fight! Don't imagine your partner to have a fight with you before he even did!

And I must admit – I can't wait to make this exercise with my son!

You cannot hate a person, when you truly understand him. The more you understand, the more you fall in love without wanting to get something from this person.

Let us recall the two most essential questions that you allegedly ask at the end of your life:

How have you expanded your capacity to love? What wisdom have you gained?

I suspect that people who strived for spiritual growth answer these questions in a different way to those who have not. Why? Because they lived their lives in accordance to the basic principles of all religions, designed to expand our capacity to love and gain wisdom. In his book, Oneness: Great Principles Shared by all Religions, Jeffrey Moses cites 65 principles that are common to a host of Holy Scriptures. And from that list, I have selected those which I regard as most relevant to the family/relationships:

The Golden Rule – Treat others as you would have them treat you

Jeffrey Moses considers this fundamental to all religions and spiritual practice. Jesus referred to the Golden Rule as "the law and the prophets", and Mohammad referred to it as "the noblest expression of all religions". Rabbi Hilel states that in the Jewish Talmud, the Golden Rule "is the whole of the Torah and the remainder is but commentary"... And Confucius, the great Chinese philosopher, deemed it "the one principle upon which one's whole life may proceed."

I believe that this rule can be followed but under one condition: mindfulness. I believe that no-one can consciously hurt themselves or another person. When we increase our mindfulness, we no longer operate like reactive machines or act according to habitual responses. We are far more likely to follow the 'Calm Down. Grow Up. Get Closer' formula, especially the calming down part. In recent publications on family happiness, psychologists have tended to offer a different interpretation of this law by advocating that it is more important to be the right partner than to find one. i.e. do your best to treat others as you would like to be treated rather than demand that they treat you in a certain way. I see it as a win-win situation on two counts: the problematic pattern is broken and I grow in a relationship by striving for the best. There are no guarantees of "success" in any family, but this single principle could highly increase our chances of a satisfying marriage. Napoleon Hill takes this concept one step further, by telling us to "think of others the way you want them to think of you". In other words, use your head to train/discipline yourself to treat people well and then see how that will be reflected in your actions.

Questions for self-reflection

Please recall a situation in which you found yourself in conflict with someone else and pause at the part when tension peaked. Before responding to their words or actions in the way that you did, take a breath and ask yourself, "How would I like them to respond to me if the tables were turned?" You will inevitably discover that you would expect them to be kinder, nicer and more understanding and respectful towards you than you were to them! Now ask yourself: "What could I do to ensure that I would offer this type of response to a similar situation in the future?"

The World is Our Family - this is what I discussed in the Social Maturity chapter. There are no others, there are no strangers, when it comes to spreading your love and compassion. In Islam, it says: "All creatures are the family of God; and he is the most beloved of God who does most good for His family."

You Reap what you Sow - this is another way of stating the Golden Rule, or rather the reason to follow it. Again, it is one of the most challenging principles to follow in our quick-fix, consumerist era, and yet the most fundamental for family happiness. In modern terms, it means you manifest in life whatever you invested in it. This was perhaps one of my greatest discoveries. Like I said in the beginning of this book, if I constantly 'invest' resentment and dissatisfaction in our marriage, create more reasons for resentment and dissatisfaction. And vice versa, if despite all the habitual demands of my ego, I invest genuine joy, gratitude and love, I shall receive it multiplied in return.

Yet, as practice shows, many partners do not know where and how to sow. All too often, we demand something that we don't even know how to give ourselves, let alone others. Here are some classic examples of demands and how they can be counterbalanced: I need him to support me - Are you supporting his needs? Do you actually ask him how you can support him or are your actions based on your assumptions? You want to be loved in a way that suits you but are you equally aware of the quality of love that he requires? What about you personally? Have you learned how to give love for yourself?

If I constantly 'invest' resentment and dissatisfaction in our marriage, I create more reasons for resentment and dissatisfaction. And vice versa; if despite all the habitual demands of my ego, I invest genuine joy, gratitude and love I shall receive it multiplied, in return.

Questions for self-reflection

As part of our homework in the Tatyana Latanska's Women's Club, we were asked to read a classic on intimate relationships - The Five Love Languages: How to Express Heartfelt Commitment to Your Mate by Gary Chapman. Its content is highly accessible and I highly recommend it to couples. After understanding the concept of the languages listed - gifts, quality time, words of affirmation, acts of service (devotion), and physical touch (intimacy) - take time to find your own language and that of your partner. That will give you the key to expressing your love, beginning with yourself. It is part of human nature to want to be loved, and to do things out of love. It is therefore important that we find the best means of doing so as early as possible if we are to fulfill these needs. As you sow small acts of kindness, so shall you reap a harvest of love and harmony. What is your language and how can you use it to express love for yourself ?

What is your mate's language and how can you best express it?

Better to Examine Thyself - I would say it's not only better, but the only way to begin living a more balanced life. Any conflict involves more than one person. I remember that when there were fights in my kindergarten, we children would always compete with each other to claim our innocence, usually be telling our teacher that someone else started it. Unfortunately, this trait continues into adulthood .We should therefore explore alternative means of resolving conflict and avoid the trap of simply laying the blame on another party. One of the most effective ways of resolving a conflict/problematic pattern is to ask yourself: "What behaviour/words of mine have caused the other person to act in this way?" This is what Hal Runkel terms the 'Grow up' step. And really contemplate on that. It increases your level of compassion and most importantly, your ability to change things simply because you cannot change others, regardless of how attractive that appears to your ego.

Judge Not - is closely related to the previous principle and should serve as a beautiful reminder of what can be achieved. Carl Rogers's influential client- based therapy is an excellent example. Instead of offering them professional advice or imposing established techniques on his clients, he simply showed his acceptance of who they were. In many cases, the impact was so profound that his clients were able to alleviate their schizophrenia symptoms. Yet, we all judge, even we family psychologists, who have trained for years to accept people the way they are. The good news is that we no longer need to feel guilty about it! This huge obstacle in our lives can be transformed into a spiritual tool if we tackle Byron Katie's Judge-Your-Neighbour-Worksheet. Instead of rejecting this natural (and potentially enlightening) tendency, we can use it to our advantage. We can judge other people in a way that makes us see how non-judge worthy/innocent they are, and through judging find out more about ourselves and our capacity to truly connect to people.

Always Speak the Truth – Throughout childhood, most of us are indoctrinated with the notion that 'honesty is the best policy'. My parents constantly encouraged me to be honest and this helped me share all kinds of things with them, despite my fear of being misunderstood or judged. But for many years, when it came to relating to others, I was terrified of expressing my true opinions. It is only now that I am able to see what was holding me back; something which I have termed: 'Imaginary, terrible things that will happen, if I speak the truth'. It was like a horror film being played in my head by my ego and one that posed so many dangerous scenarios that I couldn't even consider being honest. I therefore developed the habit of concealing my true intentions, feelings and thoughts in order to avoid imaginary punishment or adverse reactions. Imagine how hard it was to be burdened by a sack of lies which grew heavier by the year. I was still unaware that my sweetest reward would be personal integrity or that while voicing the truth carries risks, it always brings internal peace. And what could be more important?

Another aspect of speaking the truth is getting in touch with your unique inner truth, something that feels right only for you, and respecting it. In any relationship, people disagree on things. This is no bad thing but it does not mean sacrificing your own truth. In my own case, I am constantly bombarded with other people's advice on how to raise my child and from time to time, accused of doing strange things! I hear what they're saying but in the end, find peace in my own decisions, which come from my heart, not from my mind.

Be Slow to Anger - We all know how angry outbursts have destroyed many a relationship, families, countries, and even civilizations. But the opposite is also true: if we can control our anger; we have the ability to save a relationship, a soul or in extreme cases, a life. So what does it take to harness such control? Many religions would argue that the answer lies in consciousness and suggest different ways to heighten our connection with it – through prayer, meditation or Sufi whirling. 'Be Slow to Anger', acknowledges that anger is an inevitable emotion, with the subtext that it can be slowed or calmed once we learn how to control it.

Start Young to Seek Wisdom, especially when it comes to happiness in relationships. Notice how it says 'seek' and not 'receive', a phrase that is particularly pertinent to the knowledge shared in this book and barely offered in any conventional school. It usually takes a divorce, sometimes two or even three, for people to understand necessary lessons about marriage. In her recently published, The Book of a Married Woman, Kazakhstani best-selling author, Madina Baibolova, shares the wisdom she gleaned after 9 years of unhappy marriage. It is sadly the case that it sometimes takes a traumatic event to furnish us with the tools we need to dissolve illusionary programming received in childhood. And yet, this knowledge has long been freely available in numerous spiritual texts which provide guidance on how we can improve our characters. A now famous experiment was conducted in Almaty, Kazakhstan by a group of my colleagues in 2014. Prior to court hearings, they received permission from the local authorities to conduct 30 – 60 minute interviews with couples awaiting their divorce, resulting in 90% postponing or canceling their trials. It illustrates that it sometimes takes only a little information to reverse a situation if we are prepared to seek it.

Seek and Ye Shall Find – In every religion we are warned that the road to spirituality is not necessarily short and easy, nor is it ever a destination. Yet it is open and awaits everyone, regardless of how sinful they perceive themselves to be. As Oscar Wilde once said, "Every saint has a past, and every sinner has a future." I used to believe that spirituality was for other people; definitely not me. I couldn't decide whether my story made me a sinner or a saint but once I began focusing on the present rather the past, that labelling became irrelevant. I realized that in order to seek inner peace and love, I would need to journey into my inner self. Only there would I find ALL of the resources I need to fulfil my potential to share love in the spiritual sense with my family.

Pride comes before a fall – Pride is dictated by fear and always has a bitter taste. It becomes especially obvious, when you question pride-related concepts or thoughts. You will also notice that pride barely resides in the present. Instead, it involves collecting images from the past and creating new illusionary images which separate you from the future. At the end of the day, when you realize that you don't need a mind-created separation, you will fall.

Question for self-reflection

Is there any principle that strongly resonates with your inner world? If yes, what is it?

Another way I step into the "third dimension" is by acknowledging and then working through the stages of awakening presented by Joe Vitale in his audiobook The Awakening Course. Elif Shafak illustrates similar stages to be found in Sufism. I have extended these stages to apply to relationships:

1. Victimhood
2. Empowerment
3. Surrendering
4. Awakening

What are they all about?

The main characteristic of a victim is blaming, or denying responsibility for the situation in which I find myself with my partner. The main rhetoric of a victim is, "I am unhappy because you did or didn't do this or that". The main focus is the external world and how you react to it, based on programming and stories from your past. It is the utmost version of the cockroach perspective.

Empowerment is the stage when I realize that I have control over much more that I previously imagined. I start understanding the law of cause and effect; my share in conflicting or peaceful situations with my partner; my influence on negative thinking. I believe in the law of attraction and my picture of the world seems bright but I am in danger of falling into ego's trap and seeing myself as almighty. As long as my ego occupies centre stage, I cannot help but feel disappointed with my lot and will be unable to progress to the next level.

Surrendering is to understand that despite the power that I have been granted by God (higher force/Universe), there are still things beyond my control. My life would benefit from an accepting and surrendering to this higher wisdom[25]. At this stage I still strive to change my situation or my relationship with my partner by working on myself, but at the same time, begin to understand that some things cannot be changed for a reason. The difference between this stage and victimhood is the place where I come from: in the former I am struggling with my partner, while in the latter, I am struggling with my ego by teaching it to let go. It is at this stage that I can differentiate between three types of business, as cited by Byron Katie: Mine; Yours; God's and can act accordingly.

I do not get stressed about my spouse's health because that is his business! Mine is to tell him what I think and concentrate on my own health and well-being. At this stage I also see that it is not my job to rescue someone from unhealthy habits - it is theirs and God's. I also notice that I am feeling more relaxed about his health without knowing why. I leave such answers to God, or higher forces, if you will.

---

[25] The Turkish word for this is- Khikmet- our first son's middle name.

At the awakening, the highest stage, I finally reach the universal truth (halleluiah!) that nothing external, even the greatest and most desirable change in my partner, will ever bring me lasting happiness and peace. My happiness will forever depend on my ability to connect with my divine part of self; something which exists within all of us. And it is best made through connecting to the now, i.e. awakening to the third dimension. It is not the point of perfection, as I first thought, but rather, the point of experiencing inner peace despite external circumstances, or my partner's words or actions. I am still working on myself and draw my strength not from my actions but my connection with the Universe and my present moment in it. I finally get to see that I am the ocean in a drop. I am a spiritual being going through human experience. I love. And laugh!

Question for self-reflection

At which stage do you mostly find yourself? Answer without judgement!

When I try to instill the concept of spiritual maturity in my son, when he turns five, I will tell him to stop and breathe whenever he feels upset. I will ask him to notice his breathe, his hands, and the sounds and light around him, and to feel the light within him by imagining that he is filled with sunrays. He must then return to where he was standing and look around until he feels happy and confident to face anything. When he grows older, we will then meditate together. Life is simple and full of love, once you are able to stop and notice. You are love.

Questions for couples:

Do you and your partner practice any religion? How do you see your relationship working if you have different spiritual beliefs and what are your expectations regarding his or her practices?

What spiritual activities could do engage in both together and separately?

YOUR APPEARANCE IN THE REAL WORLD AND SOCIAL MEDIA

*Taking joy in living is a
woman's best cosmetic.*
Rosalind Russell

Nowadays, for millions of people, there are two distinct channels through which their appearance is presented: real life and social media. The world is obsessed with carefully constructed selfies and images posted on Facebook and Instagram. It is not my intention to debate whether this is right or wrong but rather, raise awareness of this current trend. Many of us choose to manipulate captioned pictures of ourselves in order to enhance our profiles, both professionally and socially on social networks but what is achieved by this and do the results have a significant impact on our relationships?

Far too often, I have strived to make an impression based on the belief that my most powerful tool is my appearance. This is something that I had learned from classic fairy tales and later reaffirmed by surreal images of models in women's magazines, extolling perfection through digitally manipulated images. Convinced that this is what was expected of me, I became increasingly disheartened by my non-standard body and grew depressed by the misguided perception that physical perfection was the only road to people's hearts. I would probably have continued believing this, had I not observed an interesting fact: Not all beauty queens enjoy happy relationships and conversely, not all the happy relationships include a beauty queen. In fact the very opposite is often the case! Far too many people, and especially young men and women, are obsessed by their looks. They are not bad people and nor is their natural appearance their enemy. They simply crave admiration, and approval, for the effort they have invested in their appearance.

But in the process, they forget to invest anything in the single most important quality for happy relationships: the ability to love.

I remember feeling anxious about coming to the Ukraine, for I was afraid of cruel competition from the world's most beautiful women. Little did I understand that my lack of confidence lay in a less than flattering image that I'd created of myself which meant that even if the most attractive men and women looked me in the eye and declared me the most beautiful human being on Earth, I would question their judgement. And that was shaky ground on which to build my house of hope. The only place that can ever offer you a true and stable foundation is your inner self. It is also why it is so important to spend time alone; to become self-centered.

Without that revelation, I would have kept on expecting my husband to praise my looks at every opportunity; an unrealistic demand that unmet, would have made married life tortuous.

The same goes for 'selfies' posted in their thousands, hour upon hour, by people seeking approval from others.

This chapter will concentrate on **how we can sustainably care for our appearance without damaging the psyche,** by following the principle that appearance is a tool to express ourselves, not to impress others.

I have chosen to address this subject at the end of the book for two reasons. Firstly because it provides a logical conclusion to the areas discussed in previous chapters and secondly, because I know so little about the world of fashion and beauty (is there much to know?)! The good news is that if you have got this far in the book, I am here to welcome a BEAUTIFUL new you! By now, but hopefully much earlier, you must have realized that you are amazingly attractive, just the way you are, in this moment. Things could change within a day or a month, but right now you are what you are. Please step into the third dimension and without comparison to anyone else, acknowledge your beauty!

Appearance is a tool to express ourselves, not to impress others.

I recall a famous video-experiment conducted by Shea Glover that went viral, when she told people that she was taking pictures of the things she found beautiful. The students' reactions varied but most were taken by surprise resulting in natural rather than posed smiles[26]. So I thought how great it would be if we all adopted the habit of telling ourselves we are beautiful whenever we look in a mirror and with time, gradually become accustomed to the idea? The truth is that within your head, there's a host of silent compliments waiting to burst forth and the time has come for you to let them to speak up!

Questions for self-reflection

Please stand in front of a mirror and imagine that a stranger has told you that they want to take pictures of something they find beautiful and then pay you a series of compliments.

Write yourself a letter listing 7 nice things that they could have told you about yourself. If all they said was that you were beautiful, how would you feel?

✍

1.

2.

3.

4.

5.

6.

7.

_____

_____

[26] https://www.youtube.com/watch?v=aW8BDgLpZkI

With the help of exercises from the previous chapters, you will have raised your self- esteem from within; faced your greatest fears and biggest dreams; journeyed across the borders of your usual identity; laughed and cried at yourself; become better at loving yourself and others and given yourself the confidence to become the best version of you... Whether you realize it or not, you are by far the most beautiful human being in the now! It has nothing to do with size, age, religion, gender, race, ethnicity, cosmetics, or even the size of your wrinkles or acne pores.

I hope that by now, you have also grown closer to both your own nature and to Mother Nature. As Scott Westerfeld, an American writer puts it: "Nature didn't need an operation to be beautiful. It just was." And since we are part of nature, this applies to us too. It is incredible to think how many conditions we place upon ourselves simply to feel beautiful – lose weight, eliminate wrinkles, improve our wardrobe, change our hair, increase the breast size, to name but a few! I do not know where it all went wrong; when did we start believing that we need anything to be beautiful? Perhaps we can blame the plethora of clever marketing which tricks us into buying "beautifying" products by convincing us that there is something wrong with us? When Oscart Brand investigated this theory by studying magazines such as ELLE and Cosmopolitan he was astonished to discover that 65-85% of their content was allocated to adverts and wryly concluded that they should be renamed "Product Catalogues."[27]

So if we really want to learn about fashion and beauty and benefit from real life accounts about people, rather than computer-generated bodies,[28] we should turn instead to books or talk to specialists. So-called beauty has become a

---

[27] https://www.youtube.com/watch?v=zIIKTNPP5Ts

[28] http://www.dailymail.co.uk/femail/article-2070393/H-M-putting-models-heads-generated-bodies-sell-swimwear.html

commodity that people hope to trade in exchange for love, care, admiration and respect and sadly this is prevalent in the search for relationships. When I was lecturing in vocational schools, I constantly heard girls complaining:

"Men don't fall for ugly girls. We must be beautiful."

I find three fundamental problems with this common rhetoric:

1.   Why are we treating men like objects to be manipulated into a relationship?

2.   Why do we let anyone other than ourselves determine our beauty?

3.   Who told you that beauty is created rather than rediscovered from within?

It's not about passively accepting and doing nothing about the way we look, but adopting a healthier approach. I discussed self-image in the chapter on physical maturity but this time; I will emphasize the importance of getting in touch with your beauty in the now. If you unable to see it in the moment, the chances are that it will continue to elude you, regardless of whatever conditions you subject it to. This in turn, will lead to a never-ending story of 'improvements' which in your eyes at least, can never validate the version of beauty that you are looking for.

 I have suffered from acne for the past fifteen years and during the first 10, lived in hope that it would disappear and hence, improve my life. Now here I am, almost acne –free, but has my life changed? Yes: But not because of my appearance. My life has changed because I was determined to instigate change and in fact, when I first started dating my husband, my acne was at its peak. So the true union of two people has nothing to do with appearance.

However, it is not always easy to accept that beauty starts from within when this notion is constantly contradicted by glossy magazines and TV. Even shows which promise to promote the truth, tell us the opposite. For example, the top 5 Russian TV shows on "making women more beautiful"[29] place all emphasis on styling and quick fixes and I must admit that in my early twenties, I dreamt of having someone transform my appearance on one of these programmes. And aren't we all seduced, or at least curious, by the ease at which anyone can be made to look like a model? Well, the truth is we don't know (and do we want to know?) what happens to these participants in a year or two. We want to believe in the 'happily ever after'; the part where the newly glamorous Cinderella catches her prince. The chances are that each participant will enjoy her transformed looks for a while, but unless she learns how to work on her self-image, drawn from an inner love for herself, any stylist's work will be in vain. It reminds me the lottery-winning effect: about 70 percent of people who suddenly receive a windfall of cash will lose it within a few years, according to the National Endowment for Financial Education[30]. Some authors on financial freedom claimed that they even end up in debt after three to four years.

The beauty transformation TV programmes remind me the lottery-winning effect: about 70 percent of people who suddenly receive a windfall of cash will lose it within a few years.

Questions for self-reflection

How much time AND money per week do you spend on my appearance, including:

---

[29] http://7days.ru/fashion/trends/5-samykh-populyarnykh-peredach-gde-zhenshchinam-pomogayut-stat- krasivee.htm
[30] http://time.com/4176128/powerball-jackpot-lottery-winners/

- Buying clothes and beauty products online and at the shops?

✍

- Applying and removing make-up?

✍

- Styling my hair at home and in the salon?

✍

- Selecting what to wear?

✍

- Discussing clothes with friends?

✍

- Manicures and beauty treatments?

✍

This exercise is intended to raise awareness of, rather than criticize, our investment in our appearance.

-Ask yourself every time you get ready in front of the mirror: Am I doing this out of love for myself or from fear of being judged? If you detect fear, take time to contemplate the reason before moving on to the next question,

-What would I suggest that I to wear, if I loved myself dearly and unconditionally?

-How could I combine the ritual of dressing up with developing my other 6 maturities? E.g.: listening to audio-books or experts on YouTube, affirming your qualities in front of the mirror, etc.

✍

To find out more about fashion, I consulted my friend, Vita Konovalova[31], an image therapist from Ukraine, who inspires and coaches women from different backgrounds to connect with their inner self-image. She claims that we intuitively construct an image in our minds of what we look like and all we have to do is to express it through colour, texture and fashion. These should be regarded as tools instead of dictating what we should look like, according to trends and other external influences. In order to adopt this concept, she recommends the 4 "P" formula[32], which leads us to explore, accept, love and express who we really are in terms of physical appearance.

Here is how it works. The first step – exploring – means learning about yourself; something which you will have been doing through the previous exercises in this book.

Vita suggests that you list 4-5 descriptions of yourself, including comments from others, which best represent who you are. Please be specific.

1.

2.

3.

4.

5.

Now look in the mirror and spend time learning about your shape and the colour of your skin. On the left of the page, list what you perceive to be defects, and on the right, list how

---

[31] www.vitakonovalova.com
[32] In Russian, all the words start with letter "п" - pronounced as "p". Originally it is "4П: Познай, Прими, Полюби, Прояви".

these highlight anything that pleases you. For example, Vita writes that her disproportionally wide thighs make her waistline look thinner.

✍

1.

2.

3.

4.

5.

Step two involves acceptance of your appearance. This time when you face the mirror, tell your alleged defects "I love you and am grateful for you".

The third step is showing ourselves love. Vita recommends that we follow the advice of a dear colleague Gary Chapman and begin and end each day by telling ourselves: "I love you deeply and unconditionally". In addition, you should think of 10-15 things you would like to do for yourself and then make sure that you do at least one of them daily.

The fourth step is expressing yourself through your appearance. This involves focusing on your inner self-image and on a desire to impress yourself through colour, texture and the cut of your clothes. For example, one of my inner self-images could be described as 'respectable' and I express this through wearing dark blue or black clothes of closely woven fabrics which fall below the knee.

A similar approach should be applied to how we appear in social media. Whenever I post an image, I ask myself what it is that I am striving to express. Is it based on my inner values or a fear of being judged? Am I sharing information to create an identity or to illustrate my nature?

Through Vita I met a very remarkable photographer - Taras Gegelsky[33], who helps people to see and express their natural beauty. One of his projects, the 'Psychological Portrait', aims to show the ultimate attraction of authenticity. No posing, no glamour, no excessive make-up – just a portrait of someone as they appear in the here and now. I found it tremendously empowering to work with him.

There was a moment in that photo session when I suddenly saw how beautiful I can be without a mental picture of how I should look. Gegelsky's pursuit of authenticity is contagious and I found just being around him, highly rewarding. Can you identify such people in the circles in which you mix? Think about who inspires you to be natural.

Finally, there is a specific reason why I placed appearance on the armrest of the chair. It is a part which finishes off a chair rather than something added at the beginning of its construction. You cannot determine the things that you love to do, what you should learn, expand your knowledge in, or even what exercise you should try, just by looking at your appearance. And you cannot enter a relationship with only an armrest for your chair and hope to be comfortable since after all, it is not designed to be sat on!

When I come to talk about appearance with my son, when he turns five years, I will tell him that it's always nice to look good and you should strive to look your best, but it is far more important to develop your inner beauty by loving yourself and the world. When you see beauty within, it is easy to spot it everywhere around you.

Questions for couples:

How important are social networks for your partner? And for you?

---

[33] www,gegelskiy.com.ua

How can you help your partner feel more beautiful? And how in turn, can they do likewise for you?

CONCLUSION

Romantic love is based on the notion that in order to feel complete, you need to find your 'significant other'. I have learnt through experience that this is no more than a fanciful myth and in time, you too will come to accept that you need no-one to complete you.

Byron Katie

First and foremost I want to thank you for coming on this journey. But this is not the end of the road and I look forward to receiving your feedback so that I can explore new avenues. It is my plan to organize several presentations and courses on the subject and hope that you will join my audiences and share your stories about how you befriended with your chair. Most of all, I hope that the concepts presented in this book have helped you just as much they helped me become a little kinder person. I can't wait to meet more 'chairmen' and 'chairwomen'!

It is my dream to unite all those individuals and organizations who are working on building healthy relationships within the family by embracing the following mindset:

Unconditional Responsibility: My chair is not a guarantee of a happy marriage or happy life. That's up to me. The whole chair or parts of it can disappear in a moment. My partner could walk out of my life; I could lose my job or even, like Steve Jobs, be fired from my own company. But I will not let anyone or situation can take away my self-respect and love for myself (psycho-emotional maturity); my will to exercise, no matter how slight (physical health); my passion and freedom (intellectual maturity); my ability to earn (financial maturity); my ability to make new, and maintain old, friendships (social maturity); my spiritual beliefs (spiritual maturity); and my ability to feel beautiful (appearance).

Nurturing and developing every part of the chair is a form of mental fitness that increases my peace of mind, just as physical fitness improves my physical health. "But what", I hear you ask, "will happen if my mental capacity diminishes?" Well, there is no guarantee that it won't but hopefully, specialists will be on hand to help you readjust. Otherwise, you must learn how to focus on your own mental state rather than external circumstances to secure true happiness.

Mindful Responsibility: The more attuned I am to my inner consciousness, the greater my access to happiness. As Chris

Gardner says in the film, "Pursuit of Happyness", "Happiness is spelled with an I not a Y." I stand at the beginning and the end of my own misery or joy. It does not matter where I come from and what traumas I experienced in my past. I have studied many historically significant women who managed to build happy and secure families under seemingly impossible circumstances. One of the brightest examples is a Ukrainian woman named Roxalana, later known as Hurrem Sultan. The first female slave to manage to free herself, she married her former master, Sultan Suleiman the Magnificent. Blessed with neither beauty nor a privileged background, she became renowned for her strength of character and wit, and most importantly, her role in changing the course of history of the Ottoman Empire, and thereby the world[34].

Throughout time, there have been countless women who despite their beauty, sexual power, fame, and admiration, have failed to find lasting happiness for either themselves or their partners. A famous example is Marilyn Monroe, who even has a syndrome of this unhappy state named after her.

Responsibility without sacrifice: The increase in divorce rates cannot be attributed to women's increased earning power but rather, the result of our collective consumerist approach to relationships which serves as a diversion from an innate yet forgotten desire to love ourselves and others. It is also due to our growing inability to discuss our personal ambitions. Money does not have the power to change people per say but it almost certainly amplifies aspects of our personalities. If we were unloving when we had no money, it is highly likely that wealth will make us more so. As a working woman, I do not have to sacrifice the fulfilment of my potential for the sake of my family. In other words, denial of self-realization is not a price to be paid for a happy family. It is my understanding that an integral part of self-realization is the ability to love and family should be its greatest recipient. Perhaps other

---

[34] 'The Magnificent Century' Tims Productions

women have a different view. In 'Black Milk', Elif Shafak cites many inspiring examples of female authors who have managed to combine family life with their writing and equally, prominent single writers who were happy to dedicate their lives to their craft. My key argument is that a happy family life does not depend on a happy housewife. Women have far more to offer the world, and in turn, their families, than the performance of household tasks. Husbands will often say that when they come home, they want to be greeted by a lively wife and homemade food rather than a tired, working spouse who hasn't had time to cook. And in response, I would tell them that the latter scenario is due to problems with time-management, an unfulfilling job and lack of spiritual and physical exercise, rather than women's participation in life outside the household. Delicious food is all very well but if a woman is unable to develop her mind, a couple will soon have nothing to talk about over their evening meal. And when there is no communication, love quickly fades, leaving only resentful or wearisome cohabitation.

As this book draws to a close, I have come to realize that it has chosen me, just as babies choose their parents before coming into the world. All I did was to surrender to it and let it flow through me. Some of the ideas appeared totally unexpectedly and I experienced joy and excitement akin to that moment when your infant first smiles at you. I am sharing my baby with the world but as it grows, will continue to nourish it with love and care.

I hope that this book has inspired you to read more and attend events related to the subject and above all, guided you gently towards new horizons of your relationship with yourself.

I believe by now you feel more like a chairman or a chairwoman of your life!

A Letter from your Chair

Dear Friend,

Thank you so much for reading about me and developing my concepts. I've waited for this moment for as long as I can remember. I am here to support you, to hold you, to be there for you, to love you, to calm you, and to connect you to your inner core. You cannot imagine how happy I am to serve you.

There are times when I might feel uncomfortable and so invite you to adjust me according to your taste. You are also welcome to restore parts of me whenever they become worn or broken. I don't come with an insurance policy. Please remember to refresh me with me with new ideas. I like to be acknowledged and celebrated. Let's have a small celebration right now! Just imagine you and me waltzing and partying till the sunrise! I'm so glad we've finally met and I can't wait to join you on adventures!

Before we do, please spare the time to check over my parts. On a scale from 1 to 10, 1 - being barely developed to 10 - completely developed, how would you rate my different components? I can happily exist at any stage of construction, so long as there's integrity in my making.

I have one last request - I like to stay beneath the light (of your consciousness).

With love,

Your Chair.

APPENDICES

Daily Check List

Maturity	Tracking your development
Psycho- emotional	What do I love (to do)? What are my areas of creativity? How can I best demonstrate my love? What can I do to appreciate who I am? How can I find happiness in serving other people? How can I expand my love?
Physical health	How can I nurture my health?
Intellectual	How can understanding something increase my ability to love?
Financial	How can I make money doing something I love? If I am unhappy at work, do I have the courage and means to change course?
Social	How can increase my love for others?
Spiritual	How can I grow spiritually to love and accept my place in the world around me?
Appearance	How can I appreciate and love how I look?

How Maturities Influence Each Other

Maturity/influence	Psycho-Emotional	Physical health	Intellectual	Financial	Social	Spiritual	Appearance
Psycho-Emotional	-	Love for yourself makes it easier to take of your body, your intellect, finances, friends, spiritual development and the way you look.					
Physical Health			When you are full of energy you can work harder on more maturities.				
Intellectual	Being smart helps you to process the information			better and make more effective decisions for all other maturities			
Financial	You can finance your activities in sports, conferences, retreats,				individual sessions and looks.		
Social	Having genuine friendships prolongs life, makes you connected and gives you a feel					sense of belonging.	
Spiritual	Connects the above dots and adds meaning to your life.						
Appearance	Brings you to a natural state of feeling beautiful and projecting your beauty to the external world. beauty externally						

Recommended Films and TV series

Films

Revolutionary Road (2008) (Personally my favorite one)

Eternal Sunshine of the Spotless Mind (2004) In time (2011)

Notebook (2004)

Last Night (2010)

Anna Karenina (2012) Gone with the Wind (1939) Into the Wild (2007) Cleopatra (1963)

Requiem for a Dream (2000) The Truman Show (1998) The Story of Us (1999)

Sex and the City (2008) Sex and the City 2 (2010)

TV Series

Magnificent Century (2011-2014)

Lucky Louis (2006-2007) Sex and the City (1998-2004)

Game of Thrones (2011-2017)

A Thought Questioned with the Work of Byron Katie

Here is an example of a completed worksheet referencing a common situation that frustrates some women in a relationship.

My husband should surprise me with gifts.

Is it true?

Yes.

Can you absolutely know that it's true?

Yes. It certainly appears so.

So how do you react when you believe that your husband should surprise you with gifts (and he doesn't)?

I feel sad and disappointed in him. I don't value the other things that he does for me. I cry and feel unworthy. I feel unloved. To my mind, surprise gifts would properly demonstrate his love for me. I don't acknowledge his natural means of expressing his love for me and even dismiss them as easier or thoughtless options. I can still picture the day when I returned home from giving birth in hospital, to no balloons or flowers. I erase the context in which it happened, I do shut myself down from remembering why he did not prepare it. I fantasize by running romantic movies in my head whilst stuck in the kitchen doing mundane chores. I see myself sad and unsatisfied in the future. I envy friends who receive surprise gifts from their husbands. I turn to cookies or sweets rid myself of my bitterness. I feel lonely. I still feel empty. And if I start demanding that my husband brings me presents, I feel even worse. But what's interesting, I start remembering my childhood, when I received surprise gifts from my father on big holidays. I also remember that I felt important for him only on this days, that's why I was so excited about holidays, and disregarded all other 360 days in a year. I start seeing that I am developing the same pattern with my husband: I do not see/disregard all the beautiful things that he does on the ordinary days and focus only on the holidays.

Who would you be without the thought "My husband should surprise me with gifts"?

My life would be so much lighter! I would focus on my own goals and activities instead of dwelling on this business. I would actually listen to him when he tells me that he's never been good at buying surprises for anyone and his behaviour does not reflect how he feels about me. I would be far more appreciative of the enormous support and love I receive from him every day. I would cherish all of his spontaneous hugs and kisses. I would count myself very lucky in that respect. I would see and value the fact that no matter what, he is fully committed to our marriage, which in itself is the biggest surprise gifts for me.

I would praise him more in front of my friends and colleagues. I would feel more loved and connected to him. I would see that one of the surprises he brings to our relationship is how quickly he is willing to understand and forgive. I would see that a surprise gift doesn't have to appear on special occasions or when I think I need it but rather, when I least expect it.

Turnarounds: For each turnaround find three examples what can be true/truer than the original statement, and select one that sounds best for you.

Turnaround #1: I should present myself with a surprise gift.

In this situation, I can make a gift of listening to myself and noticing what's going on in my head before verbally attacking my husband or berating myself. I should make a gift to me in the form of asking my husband whether he can provide something I wanted and accept whatever his answer. I can gift myself an overdue new hairstyle or make up and achieve an element of surprise in the result.

Turnaround #2: I should give him something in surprise.

I can make a gift of receiving his love in whatever form he feels comfortable with. It will be quite a surprise for him, for recently my response has been one of disinterest and disappointment. I can give him the gift of spontaneity by engaging in a slow dance wherever we are. I can give him the gift of fun by taking silly pictures of us together.

Turnaround #3: My husband shouldn't give me surprise gifts.

In reality, it's not something that comes naturally to him and the last thing I want is to receive a gift bought not from the heart but from fear of reprisal. I would rather receive something given with genuine intent even if that only happens once in a blue moon. After all, we have committed to a lifetime together. I shouldn't need to take his lack of surprise gifts as an excuse to work harder at our relationship and only then, try to be more loving and giving. He shouldn't be expected to present me with gifts because it's not something he was contracted to do when we got together.

Notes